**JOE WHITE**

QUESTAR PUBLISHERS, INC.

SISTERS, OREGON

# WHO ARE MY REAL FRIENDS?

FIFTH PRINTING, 1992



Originally titled *Surviving Friendship Pressure*
Based on *Friendship Pressure*, © 1983 by Joe White,
and published by Operation Challenge

Printed in the United States of America

International Standard Book Number: 0-945564-40-6


Questar Publishers, Inc.
Post Office Box 1720
Sisters, Oregon 97759

# CONTENTS

*To my brothers*

*Bob and Bill*

*whose loyal friendship I'll prize forever*

# A FOREWORD . . .

## BY AMY GRANT

*Friends* . . . It's funny how your feelings about a word can change over the course of a few years.

I remember a time when we chose our friends by what toys they had, or who had the best slumber parties, or who was boy-crazy and who wasn't. I don't recall that we had heavy talks or anything back then — we were just friends.

It's hard to tell when the changes began. None of us changed at exactly the same time, or at exactly the same pace, but slowly the ties of friendship went from just the "doing stuff together" closeness to needing to really talk...to be known inside.

My next-door neighbor from the second grade on (until I left home to marry Gary) was a girl named Scottie. We were in the same grade, we rode the bus together to school every morning, and we each had three older sisters. On top of that we were friends. Every day we played. During the summers we'd camp out in my backyard, and all winter long we'd play over at her house in the den. We got each other in and out of trouble for years. Together we decided when and where we would experience our first kisses with our grade school boyfriends. A few years later we discussed our first dates. Scottie used to say that if she weren't around to take care of me, my head would get loose and fall off.

Of course, there were hard, emotional times too. Times of trial and error, and trying to figure out right from wrong. I remember the one time in high school when I went out and drank myself sick. It was Scottie who helped change my attitude about that stuff. Our true friendship came through when we convinced each other that the harmful side of life wasn't what we needed to be truly happy. She helped me grow up a little as a result of that night.

I bring up all of these memories to make a point: A true friend is a person whom *you* choose to give your time, your love, your thoughts, and your dreams. You don't always feel the same about everything — but you must never let your opinions outweigh your love. You stand by each other, you learn to forgive each other, and most importantly you bring out the best in each other. You guard carefully the confidences you share, because your trust in each other is the bond that will always hold you together.

It all sounds so simple. Unfortunately, preaching and practicing are two very different things. But I believe that with God's love and His presence in our lives and in our hearts we can learn to be the best of friends to one another.

That is my prayer for all of us,

Amy Grant

Amy Grant

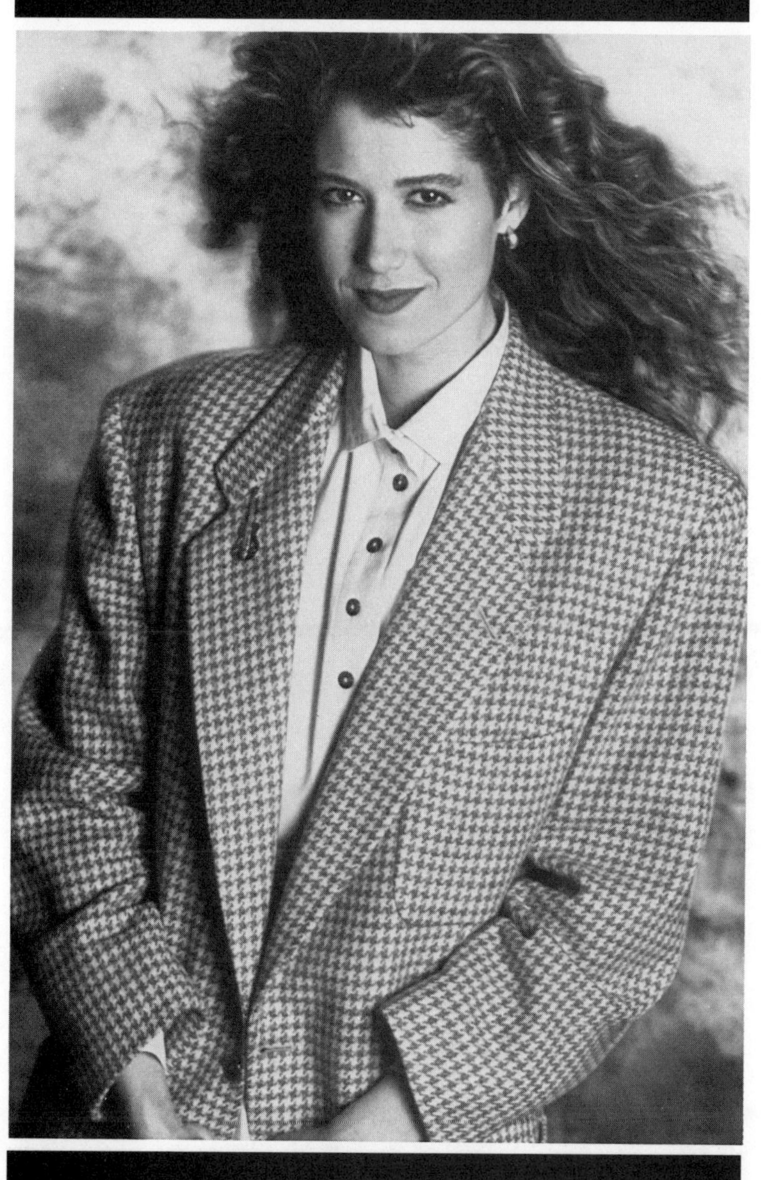

Amy Grant

Michael W. Smith

# A FOREWORD...

## BY MICHAEL W. SMITH

You can't choose your parents. You can't choose your brothers or sisters either. In fact, there are a lot of things in life you cannot choose.

But you can choose your *friends.*

I believe there is an empty place in each one of us that God has created to be filled by very special people called friends. Being a friend — a good friend who can help fill that empty place in someone else — is an art. It is attainable by us all, but it requires a lot of time and effort...and love.

The greatest friend who ever lived was Jesus — and, fortunately, the gospels give us His words of wisdom on friendship. For instance, Jesus says in John 15:13, "Greater love has no one than this, that one lay down his life for his friends." What more can you say — but what does it really mean? It must mean that being a friend could be the hardest role you'll ever play.

I know in my own life it sometimes means talking on the phone late at night to a brother who's hurting, after I've spent a long day in the studio. Or it may mean going one direction for the sake of a friend when the crowd's going the other.

But I'll have to admit that the rewards of friendship far outweigh the hassles. It's such a joy to have someone to hear your heart, someone to love you as you are, someone to laugh and cry with. A true friend is a gift!

Jesus says He chose His disciples as His friends, and that He told them *everything* about Himself — what a freedom it is to be able to bare your soul and to be loved for it.

"A lifetime's not too long to live as friends."

Michael W. Smith

Chapter 1

# WHATEVER HAPPENED TO FRIENDSHIP?

The well-worn, one-mile path I took from elementary school to my home followed a fairly direct route through backyards and vacant lots. But at one point, I always took a major detour. It was to my friend's house. "Me and my friend" made quite a pair, and we were always together: two blond, mischievous schoolboys in T-shirts and Levis.

He taught me to tie my shoes. I taught him how to shoot marbles. We could laugh at anything! I knew what he was doing any time of the day or night. I lived for Friday night so I could spend the night at his house.

But as we grew into our high school days, peer pressure drove a sudden but lasting wedge into our relationship. Now I've seen him only twice in the past fifteen years. What happened to our friendship? I wish I could say.

Good friendships in junior high and high school seem to slip away so quickly, often because of peer pressure. Where did the peer pressure begin? And

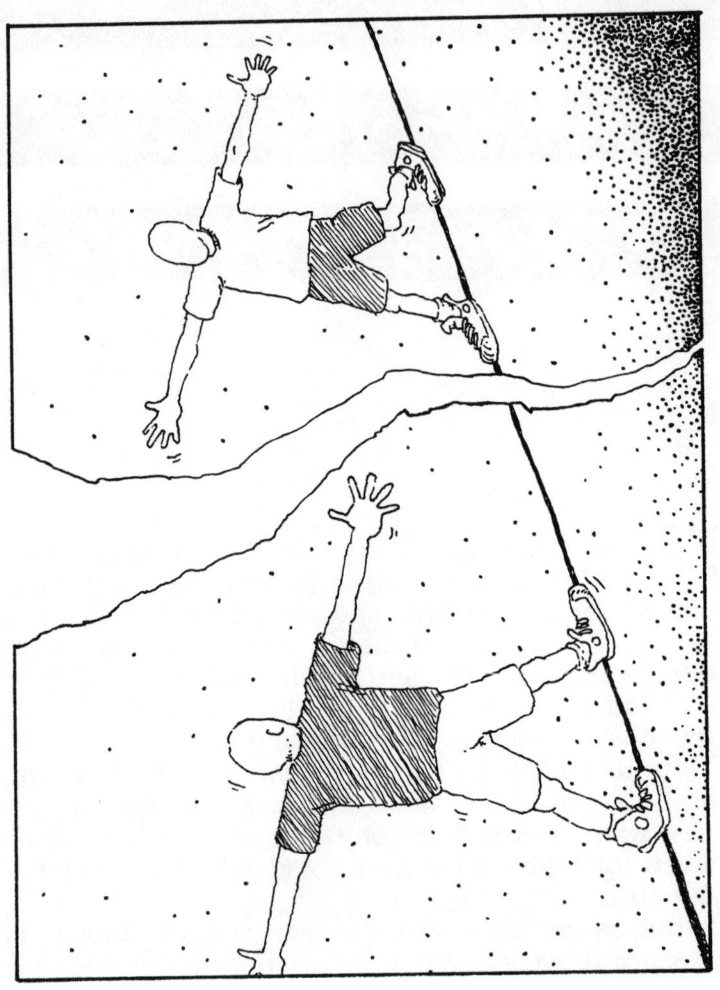

why, WHY do so many best friends rip each other off by leading one another into stuff that brings so much hurt and shame and wrecked self-image?

Recently a 16-year-old girl wrote to me,

> When I was fifteen I lost my most precious gift that I had to a football player that I did not even know. My best friend had set us up. She told me she had lost hers to the very same guy. It's been about a year and so far I've willingly given myself to eight guys. I knew it was wrong but I went ahead and did it anyway. I want to be happy and loved. I am so miserable because of what I've done. Why did my friend get me into this?

I get hundreds of letters every year with much the same story: "My friend got me into this." It kills me to see what teenagers today do in the name of friendship. I thought friends were supposed to really care for each other! I thought a best friend was someone who always wanted the best for you!

Today there are four to five million full-blown teenage alcoholics in America. They'll never know total freedom again. Because of their addiction, tens of thousands of them in the future will inflict abuse on their loved ones, and suffer divorce, and even face prison sentences. Almost all of our fellow teenagers caught in this tragic trap were introduced to their first drink by "a friend."

Missy lives in Louisiana. She was "straight" and a happy girl. Her "friends" couldn't stand it, so they poured Everclear (alcohol) into her punch at her senior party. She ended up that night wasted and totally embarrassed for some of the things she did. Her friends laughed about it for days.

Every forty-five seconds another American teenager becomes a "hopeless" drug addict. As with alcoholism, the results are tragic. I have worked with teenage friends who come to me begging for a way out of their addiction. With tracks up and down their arms, they've become a pitiful sight. Unable to keep a job, they're compelled to do anything for the next fix.

As one 17-year-old wrote me,

Thinking of days past when getting that fix was all that mattered, stealing, lying, deceiving, was all that was in my disillusioned mind. Going back to that time in my mind makes me sick. I can't believe I was there. It was all for that unrealistic high.

"Going back to that time in my mind makes me sick." Looking back is one thing. But it's a different story on the front end, when the people you're around are putting on the pressure —

*"Turn on with me, Baby!"*

*"Come on, man, are you gonna let a little fear of getting caught keep you from having fun?"*

*"What are you — chicken or something?"*

*"Hey, how's a little pot going to hurt you?"*

Did you know that almost every drug addict began doing drugs with a joint? None of them began their first trip thinking they'd end up addicted or overdosed! They all felt like they had it under control...for a while. And almost every "first joint" is pushed by "a friend."

Last summer a teenager from Kansas wrote me her own personal version of the familiar story:

There's something you've got to know about - this past year has not been easy for me. Somehow I got mixed in with the <u>wrong friends</u>. They were always partying.

First it was drinking- that led to pot- that led to speed, acid, and angel dust. Although I only did LSD and PCP one time each, it was one to many. It was an experience I'll never forget. I actually thought I was going to die. It was awful. My friends said by getting high my problems would go away. Well, that wasn't true at all. I realize that now. I feel so ashamed for what I did because I knew it was wrong and I did it anyway. The pressures on my life were tremendous (so I thought). One of my closest friends shot herself in the stomach with a .22. Luckily she lived and is doing fine now. It seemed like everyone was yelling at me and no one cared so I took a razor blade to my wrist. After that I realized I really didn't want to die, I guess I just wanted someone to know how I was feeling.

I wonder what kind of friend played a part in messing up for the first time the 19-year-old who sent me this letter:

When I was in the midst of my drugs and fooling around, I

thought I had it all together. I really believe that I could pull out of it whenever I wanted. I was just enjoying it for the time being. Boy, was I wrong. First, I would only get drunk. That resolution did not last long at all. I began to get high on pot on the weekends, then before school, then in lunch. Of course, I never believed I would get involved with qualudes and cocaine, but sure enough, I did. My school work went straight down and so did all my friends. I put an extra stress on all because eventually it hit all the ones involved, even the straight "A" students. Man, my family life was the worst. I hated being there. They were an added hassle.

They couldn't understand me, I thought. I was really the mixed-up one, not them. The pain I put them through was the worst agony they have ever experienced. I mean that. I was so self-centered. I didn't care about anyone. How could I when I was drunk and driving my friends around? Or even to pass my friends a drink or joint!

Most of my old friends are so messed up now. They're addicts or dropped out of school. These are the ones that I always thought would be the most successful. Some of them died. Yeah, it's just a really fun life, huh? Half the time I was grounded or living in a series of lies to my family and teachers. If there wasn't some type of wildness in our evening it was a drag. Gosh, we always talked about we didn't want God because He takes away our freedom, but a wild life was what I was a slave to. I would stop for awhile, but it never failed-

I always started again. I would steal money from my parents or friends if I had to. To me—my life was great and I really thought I had it together. No way! If I needed chemicals and alcohol to make me happy, that is so sad!

A 16-year-old wrote me the following letter. Where was a truly good friend when she most needed one?

You asked me if I was off the drugs, and the answer is still yes. I would never go back to that for anything in the world. I thought that drugs were helping me, but all they were doing was tearing me up. My grades dropped from A's to D's. I lost all of my friends. I tried to commit suicide several times (and almost succeeded). I ended up in a psychiatric hospital. And the worst of it was that I lost my family. When I look back at all of this, all I can do is cry. I remember all of the guilt and hurt feelings that I had. I can remember lying in the intensive care unit after I had taken an overdose. They had me all hooked up to different machines trying to keep me alive. I remember thinking at that time,

*I wish they would just let me die.*

A teenager with whom I was really close was turned on to her first joint by a friend six years ago. Her last letter to me this spring shocked me with the tragedy of "friendship."

*I made promises I tried very hard to keep. But I fell from them. But something happened a few weeks ago that changed my whole mind around. I saw my life. I saw Satan. He laughed at me. I had a very bad high. One that scares the life out of you. If I tried to explain in this letter I would lose you, really* lose myself. But take my word, I met Satan. Just imagine, I sat in a room so high I couldn't move from the chair. He was there and it might have been the drugs. But whatever it was, it was real and it happened to me. I need a $500 loan. I can't get it from my family because they don't understand what I did with all my money I made from work. I can't tell them I shoot $190 a week in dope. The sharks are putting pressure on me to pay the loans back. The pressure is intense. My friends walk on people to feed their arms and they hate themselves for it but they do. They hit a rut so big they only sink deeper I have used people to put some crud in my arm. I have left all bills unpaid. So wham! Reality!

Whatever happened to friendship?

I hope that together we can find the answer. □

*Chapter 2*

# GIRLFRIENDS AND BOYFRIENDS

One of the real highlights of my teenage years was having a special girlfriend to talk to, to go places with, to trust in, and to laugh and cry with. It's almost funny to relive some of the times we shared, like the time we bawled together when my old black dog ran away. (It was serious, man — I loved that dog!) When she lived in a different state, I'll never forget chasing the postman around town hoping I could get an early start on another exchange of love letters.

When you call a girl your "girlfriend," you're saying a mouthful (and I'm sure it's the same with a boyfriend too). You're saying, "I think you are a special lady. To me you're one in a million. I really do have a feeling for you like no one else."

**I've had the same girlfriend now** for the past seventeen years. She's been my wife for fifteen of those years. I can easily say I love her more today than I ever have before. True love is like that! It never ends.

I was on the road for a month not long ago. I stayed homesick most of the time. At the peak of my lonesome trip an old song came on a teenage friend's stereo. It was the Commodores singing "Three Times a Lady." The song jerked out my tears as only Lionel Ritchie can do. I played it over several times and cried with each refrain — "You're once, twice, three times a lady...and I love you..." That's what she is to me. You couldn't pay me a billion dollars to hurt her, to talk behind her back, or to do something that would spoil her reputation.

I called her my girlfriend for eighteen months before I could also call her my wife. I told her I loved her. Protecting her, respecting her, building her trust, developing a friendship — these were my goals for our relationship during that time.

**There's a teenage tragedy** these days — a nightmare reality to you, to me, and to our teenage friends. Instead of making you smile, when the topic of conversation turns to memories of past boyfriends and girlfriends, you'd better get ready for a heartbreaking account.

Here are a few truly tragic stories that have been shared with me by young friends from ages thirteen to twenty-five:

I was at a party two years ago and I really liked this person. Everyone had been drinking, including me - I was doing everything to let this guy know that I was alive. So he told me that he really liked me. He wanted to go all the way, but I wouldn't let him. Then he would make out with me, go down my shirt and run off to someone else and get something off them. I still kept trying to get him to notice me and again he would come back to me and then to someone else. So finally everyone had gone from the party and he started pushing me again. Finally I gave in. I felt like trash. He got what he wanted, leaving me to believe he liked me, but he never did.

"He told me he liked me" — that's the number one lie in the teenage world today. I've looked into so many crying eyes lately because a guy told a girl (or a girl told a guy) "I like you" or "I love you," when all they really meant was "I want you to satisfy this urge I've got and what I want right now is more important to me than you as a person."

Unfortunately it gets worse. So much worse. The following letter came from a bewildered university student.

I can't tell you how much I want to relive the past six months of my life. I've always wanted to be a 'good girl'. Most guys wouldn't ask me out because they knew I would not drink or 'put out'. I dated the same guy my junior and senior year in high school and I can look back at that relationship now and smile. We had a lot of good times and he treated me like a really important person. I broke that relation-off because I felt guilty about the times we would spend making out. Once he got mad at me and said that after two years he deserved something. In college I fell in love with Jim. This was the guy I was going to spend the rest of my life with. I was 19 years old, he was 22. Up to this point our phipical relationship was the most beautiful thing that had ever been experienced. I loved Jim and he loved me—no doubt—we still agreed that sex was for marriage and we'd wait. That's not to say we never were tempted. We were all too familiar with each other's bodies. He gave to me, I gave to him. I thought the phipical was just an expression of our love. Something happened to the two of us, I'm not real sure what, but I broke up after about two months. Then I met Bobby. I trusted him to know how far we could go without making love. He was in the driver's seat. He was also insecure, he would tell me over and over how he loved me, how he was sure that I didn't love him as much as he loved me. It was then that I set out to prove it. I was his—110% his. The first time we made love, I had no idea what was going on. After-wards he didn't speak, he passed out. I was *so* alone. I've never hated myself more. But it *was* done, my virginity was gone. Never could I get it back. It didn't matter after that, sex be-came an everyday occurance. My only fear was losing Bobby, he was the first and even if he treated me bad (and there were those times) I was going to do anything I could to hang on to him. Slowly we drifted apart. He wanted to go out with other girls. I loved him and he fooled me into thinking he loved me, too. The day I left for the summer we made love—yeah it was fun—but it was just actions. That same evening he told me he was going to see other people. I went through misery the next ten days being away and knowing I was carrying Bobby's child. I wasn't real sure, but I knew something was up. How was I going to explain this to Bobby? Then I began to scheme, I got excited and thought, sure, he'll want to get married. Finally I had him and if not him I had a part of him anyway. I wouldn't have an abortion, that was out of the question, I'd either marry Bobby or run off and have the child myself. Funny how Bobby controlled my mind. I told him one night after we had made love down in his basement. I thought since he was so in love with me that now was the time to break the news. He really lost it -- he got all defensive and said that there was no possible way he could marry me and that he didn't even want to. I got scared and told him I was just kidding. He breathed a sigh of relief but remained cold. It was not too long after that I told him the truth and had the pregnancy confirmed by a doctor. Bobby had stuck by his guns about not marrying me and said if I kept the child we were through. At that point I was helpless. I wanted more than anything to talk to my Mom, but I could have talked to her. Bobby stuck by me long enough to make sure I had the operation. He called me every day or wrote and made me feel like he still cared. I went in that day by myself to do the one thing I was most against. I talked to Bobby that night and then he took off. He stuck around long enough to make sure I got rid of the evidence then left me on my own. I can't explain the feelings I have inside me now. I've never thought less of myself or felt more like trash. How could I have been so naive? I loved him, but he never knew the meaning of the word. I still have nightmares and at times I hate myself, abortion is much, much deeper than the scraping of that uterus lining. It involves the destruction of one's whole being, the loss of any self respect and *saddest of all a guilt-ridden existence.*

She's certainly right about abortion's deep destruction. Consistent with the kind of effect sin always has, abortion has been shown to leave mental and emotional scars on the aborted child's father, as well as on the mother. *Time* magazine, for instance, reported the results of a study by a prominent sociologist who looked at a thousand abortion cases over a ten-year period. He found that "abortion is a great unrecognized trauma for males, perhaps the only major one that most men go through without help." Another leading counselor and psychologist noted that "abortion is one of the major death experiences that men go through. It resurrects very important, very primitive issues, memories and feelings."

**For some reason,** leading "friends" through experiences that will break their minds, their hearts, and their bodies seems at the moment like such a kick, a thrill, and a high. But later it becomes a nightmare. When I talk to kids about how to treat each other with true friendship and respect, and about the hurt and pain and suffering that's caused when we fail to do that, there are always those who write it off and say, "Those are a bunch of ancient laws made up by society. They're not relevant anymore."

But the letters you're reading in this book aren't from "society." They're from teenagers and college students just like you, from across America. And all around you are thousands of heart-breaking stories just like them. They all begin with someone building up a false trust in another teenager by calling him or her a "friend." Then, time after time, that insincere commitment becomes the biggest fraud in the school, and another victim is left to suffer by the way-side.

Don't you think we've suffered enough? □

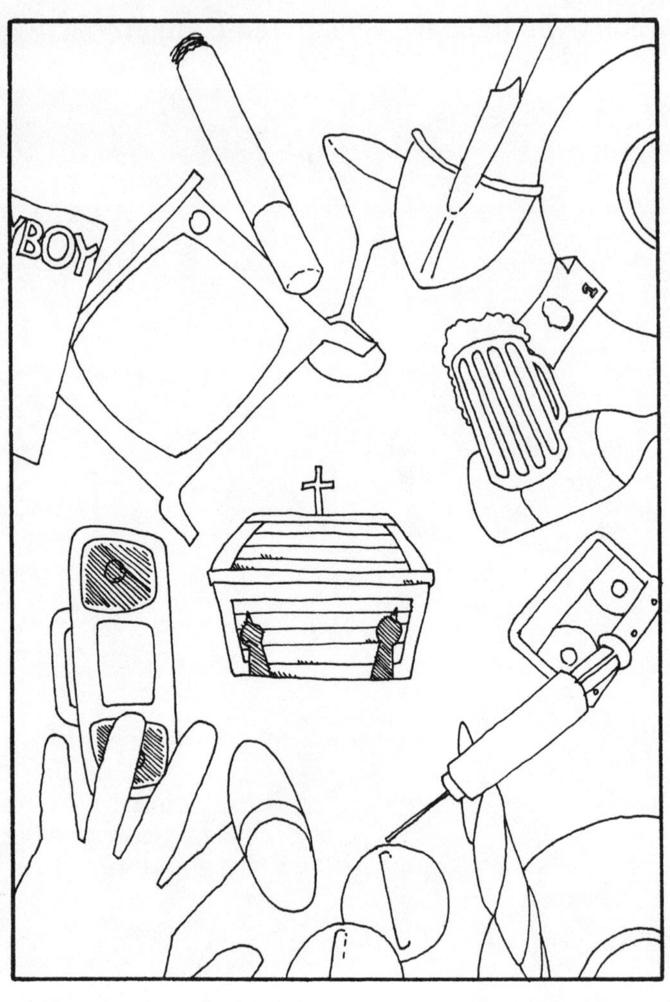
YBOY

Chapter 3

# DISCOVERING A BURIED TREASURE

Today's generations are caught in a whirlwind — a fast-paced, quick-and-easy, thrill-a-minute, if-it-feels-good-do-it movement. Every time you turn your head, someone is telling you a new idea on how to get high or how to get a new sexual thrill out of someone.

It's amazing how the beer commercials on TV (of which the average American teenager sees thousands by the time he or she is eighteen) never show you pictures of the messed-up alcoholic or the car wreck where some little child was brutally slaughtered by a drunk driver. (This became a tragic reality when it happened to my best friend's little daughter.)

It's equally amazing how the attractively suggestive (or more-than-suggestive) sexual encounters on TV (the average 18-year-old has seen between 60,000 and 100,000 of them — and the vast majority are in a setting outside marriage) almost never let you in on the indescribable pain caused by a million unwanted teen pregnancies each year.

**You don't have to be** a creative genius to see the fraud and hypocrisy in this money-making disease that is controlling the drug traffic and television brainwash! It leaves us victims of a set of "revolutionary new ideas" that are wiping out any choices for true happiness and lifetime fulfillment in today's teenage population.

You don't have to be a creative genius either to see the wisdom of planting both feet on the ground and shouting, "STOP! I've had enough of this trash!" Then you can take time to see a certain man, and to read his love letter to you that spells out in loving detail the formula for successful, happy friendships — where commitments are true, where you bring out the best in each other, and where the memories of your time together will make you smile for eternity.

The man I'm speaking of has been slandered, jeered at, and laughed at. Since the day he was born, he's been the subject of dirty jokes and violent language. Yet he remains the most intimately attractive man who ever lived. He's history's cornerstone, and he wrote the book on popularity. He was a teenager, and is well acquainted with peer pressure and temptation. He knew what it felt like to be rejected by all his "friends" in his hometown. He has dried more tears and mended more broken hearts than anyone who has ever lived. He is the best friend any guy or girl could ever have.

But he is more than that. His name is Jesus Christ. Yes, in His life on earth He was all man — as rugged and strong as any athlete. He laughed and had a great sense of humor. He cried when His heart was broken. But He was also all God. He was the "visible image of the invisible God." He died solely because of His claims of being God, and His offer of God's forgiveness for the mistakes of those who would dare to follow Him.

Today He remains the most outstanding, revolutionary figure in all of history. Even Mohammed said of Him, "Jesus is a greater prophet than I." The earth revolves around His life. His life and resurrection have been proven through exhaustive research by historians, archaeologists, attorneys, doctors, and scientists. One leading scientist stated on television that he had once acknowledged no higher authority than science itself, but now had concluded through careful scientific research that Jesus Christ was indeed who He claimed to be. "Now," he said, "I get down on my knees."

Jesus Christ originated true friendship and He wrote the all-time best-selling love letter on how to make it happen in your life. His love letter is probably in your house somewhere. It is called the Bible, and to me its words become sweeter every day. (If you don't have one, you can get one free by writing to me in care of the publisher of this book.)

In the Bible, Jesus made some great statements about friendship, such as these words in John 15:13 — "Greater love has no one than this, that one lay down his life for his friends." Jesus then laid down His life to prove that He meant it.

He also said, "You are My friends if you love Me and live as I want you to live. I don't call you slaves...I call you My friends..." (see John 15:14 -15).

His book also contains a severe warning to those who are lying to each other in the name of friendship: "God's will for you is to be pure in your body and in your mind. I want you to take care of the body God has given you and protect it from sexual sin. *Don't wrong your friend* in this manner because God is the avenger of such things. I am giving you solemn warning" (see 1 Thessalonians 4:3-6).

**Jesus has two basic things** to say about real friends:

① Real friends make you happy.

② True friendship is really <u>love</u>.

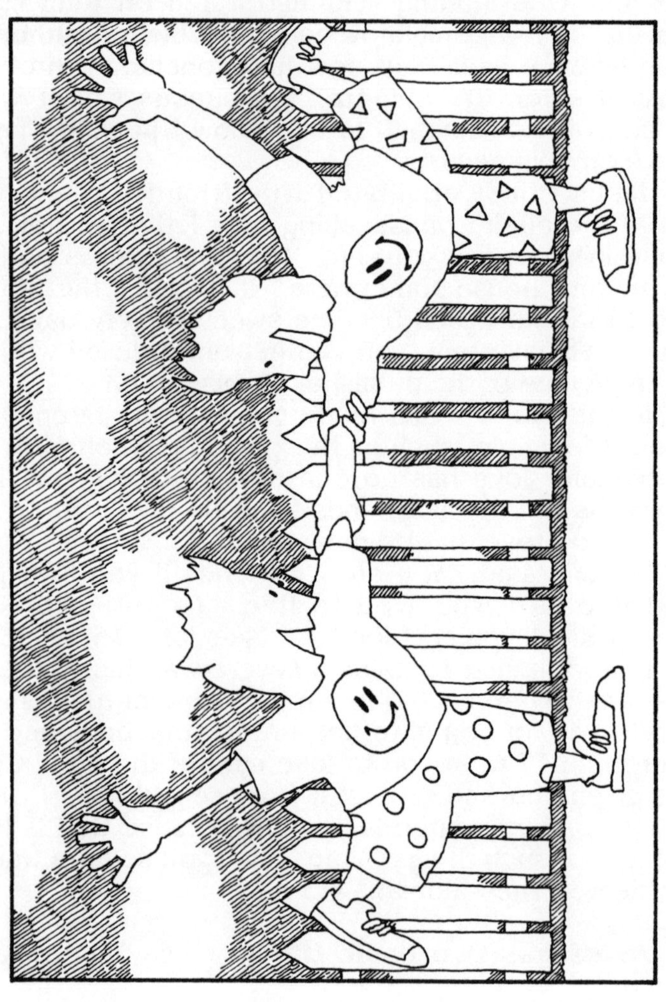

Chapter 4

# I JUST WANT TO BE HAPPY

He was Sally's oldest brother, and this was his second time to get busted for possession of illegal drugs. Just a year before, she had watched him go through a trial and a probated sentence.

Now the narcotics agent had found the stuff growing in their backyard. Sally and her parents knew Steve was on his way to jail.

For four years Steve had been consistently tearing the family apart. Now it had all fallen in on him. His family was in an uproar. His father was pressing for Steve to get out of the home. His mother was simply hysterical.

As the police approached their home to take Steve away, he burst into Sally's room. With tears flowing down his cheeks, he pleaded with his little sister: "Sally, all I want is to be happy. I just want to be happy...*I just want to be happy!"*

It's a cry that could come from the lips of any teenager I've ever met: I JUST WANT TO BE HAPPY!

I believe the discovery of happiness is found in

real friendship. That's the ancient truth that originated almost two thousand years ago when Jesus Christ lived it and taught it so clearly, but it seems to be fading rapidly today.

I'm still seeing great examples of that old truth, and I want you to know that *you* (yes, YOU!) can have it, and know it, and feel it, and experience it if you'll truly put your heart into the next few pages of this book.

Happiness is a reality.

It is found in real friendship.

You can begin a new experience in happiness today.

**I've had the privilege** of talking to thousands of teenagers and university students about friendship and happiness. I asked several hundred to write down what real friendship meant to them. The majority of them were in full agreement about it. I'll quote a few of their responses that best convey what almost all of them seemed to be saying:

> A friend is someone who is truly loyal to you and wouldn't do anything to hurt the other mentally or physically. *(Bill, age 15)*
>
> A friend is someone who will always stick by you and never make you do things you don't want to. He is loving and caring and will always have something kind and encouraging to say. *(Jason, 14)*
>
> The kind of friend that I would like to have would be someone who always encourages you, who is always your friend no matter what happens to you. A friend is honest and isn't snobby. *(Alice, 16)*
>
> A friend is someone who is always on your side, someone who cares, someone who thinks you are number one. *(Kevin, 19)*

A friend is someone who can be trusted, someone who cares, someone to turn to when in need, someone I can share prayer requests and hurts with. *(Brett, 20)*

A friend is a person who would never let me down and would always be there to lift me up. A brother or sister in Christ who will never double-cross me and would die for me as I would for him or her — that's a true friend in Christ! *(Angie, 19)*

A friend is someone you can trust, someone who can make you laugh, someone who will like you as you are, someone you can have fun with, and someone who will try to better you. *(Paula, 14)*

A true loyal person who will always take time for you and shows they care. Who loves Jesus and you. *(Tracy, 15)*

A friend is someone who loves me for me — takes the good and the bad. A friend supports and encourages me to be the best I can be — and knows that the only way to be the best is through a relationship with Christ. *(Danny, 16)*

A friend is someone who is willing to say, "I need you" or "I care for you," who loves you even when you mess up or hurt them; a companion; a listener. *(Craig, 17)*

A friend is someone who will listen to your thoughts and try to help you with your problems. They don't make fun of you. It is someone you can trust. *(Julie, 15)*

A <u>friend</u> is a person who is never rude and does not lie and helps you when you're sad and never talks behind your back and always sticks up for you and gives no peer pressure. *(Barb, 14)*

Someone I can trust — someone I can be with always — someone I can love forever. *(Randy, 16)*

A <u>friend</u> is a person who you can get along with; you can share something with them without fear of it being told. Someone who lifts you up when you're down. *(Susan, 13)*

Without <u>friends</u> there is no happiness. *(Michelle, 19)*

A <u>friend</u> is someone whose love is unconditional, whose giving is constant, and whose commitment is unbreakable. *(Jeff, 21)*

A <u>friend</u> is loving and kind. They can be trusted and depended upon. They don't mislead you or hurt you. They really care about you. They're always your friend. *(Greg, 18)*

I believe that <u>friendship</u> is one of the biggest things in my life. And the friendship I honor most is my friendship with Jesus Christ. *(Carla, 18)*

A <u>friend</u> is someone who during hard times can put a smile on your face and make everything seem better, yet a friend is also someone who will celebrate your victories with you without jealousy. *(Ginger, 16)*

A true <u>friend</u> is one who will not try to lead you into sin. He is also one who you can trust and have fellowship with. This friend accepts you as you are, and he never tries to change you. *(Sam, 16)*

A friend is someone who cares about you and likes you as you are; someone who doesn't pressure you into doing things you don't want to do; someone you can trust and be able to tell things to. *(Peter, 14)*

A true friend listens to problems, helps solve your problems, talks you into the right things to do and directs you toward Christ. *(Mark, 15)*

A true loyal person who will always take time for you and shows they care. Who loves Jesus and you. *(Tracy, 15)*

Being a friend means accepting a person as they really are. It means showing a person how much you care by just being yourself. My best friend helped me to find the Lord. Without her I never would have made it. I am so glad I found Him with her help. *(Sibyl, 16)*

Friendship means love — friendship means caring — friendship means truth — friendship means God. *(Paul, 16)*

A friend is someone who you can always turn to no matter what the situation is, or when it is. It is someone who will never talk about you or turn on you. They are always honest, caring, kind, considerate, thoughtful, and giving you unconditional love always. They will listen to all of your problems and share their joys and traumas with you. To me a friend is Jesus Christ. A best friend! He is all the things above, and more. *(Kenneth, 19)*

**When you call someone your friend**, you are giving that person the highest compliment you could give. You're saying, "You know, you really make me happy."

And you're saying even more. You're saying, "You can trust me. Don't be afraid to turn your back on me or leave town because I'll never intentionally let you down."

Finally, when you call someone a real friend, you're saying "I love you" — because *real* friendship is love. □

## Chapter 5

When you say love, you've said it all. That four-letter word is so powerful! It can heal or hurt more than any other word ever spoken.

Just before Jesus gave His greatest statement about friendship, He said, "This is My commandment, that you love one another, just as I have loved you" (John 15:12).

Inspired by God, a man named Paul wrote "Love is the greatest." He then went on, in one of the most famous Bible passages (1 Corinthians 13), to pass that beautiful word love through a prism of light. Conveying thoughts that are unmatched in their beauty, he described several of love's powerful qualities. I want to touch on a few of those qualities that relate most directly to the friendships in your life today.

**Love (real friendship) is patient.** It isn't pushy or forceful.

How many times have you seen "friends" trying to

shove a beer or a pill or a joint down someone's throat? How many "friends" have said, "I'm so tired of waiting for you to change — get with it!"? How many boyfriends and girlfriends have hurt each other by saying, "Okay...<u>show</u> me <u>now</u> that you love me — I can't wait until we're married"?

One of the most heartbroken girls I've ever met wrote me this tragic personal story last week:

Our relationship moved fast from that of friendship to engagement. He wanted to get married so bad and was looking for a woman to marry and he didn't believe in long engagements. I did and I thought I was smart but also I was afraid of losing him if I put him off so I agreed to a very short engagement and a very quick wedding. About a week before it was time for me to leave to be away for a month we

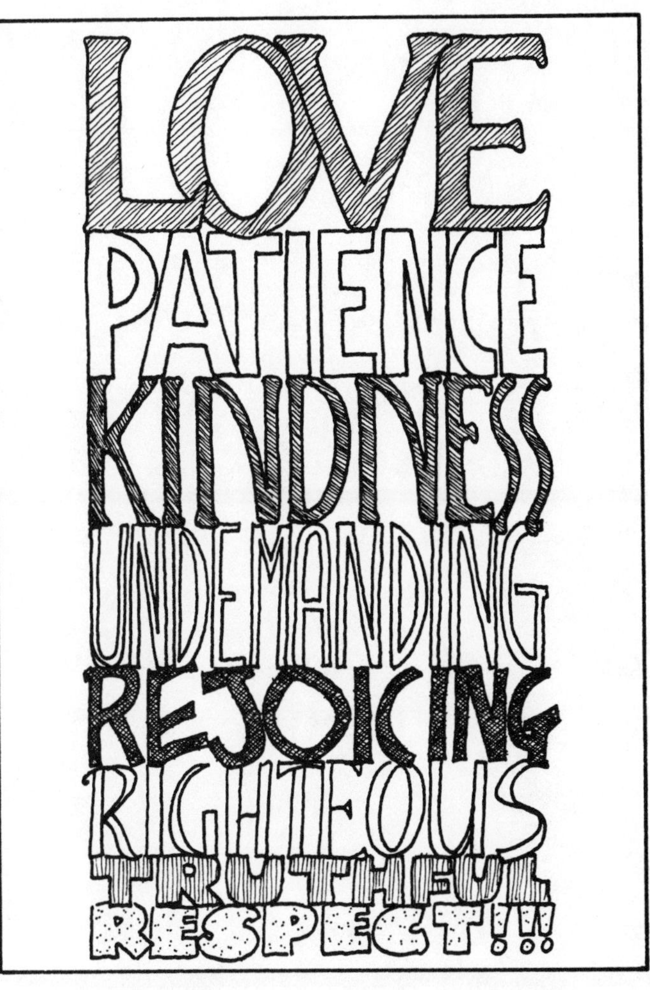
LOVE
PATIENCE
KINDNESS
UNDEMANDING
REJOICING
RIGHTEOUS
TRUTHFUL
RESPECT!!!

decided on a wedding date two months away. I was at his apartment. We were just talking and I was thinking about how to fix the apartment up. He had fixed himself a mixed drink and me one too but I was having trouble drinking it because I was afraid of liquor. Everything was really nice until a little before midnight when I decided to leave. The whole evening he kept trying to get me to marry him the next day. I kept saying August was fine and he kept saying he'd make me agree to marry him the next day and he thought he'd just start the marriage now. Next thing I knew he was all over me and so aggressive. I kept telling him to stop, I needed to go home, kept fighting him, but he wouldn't let up. He was so strong and I was petrified but I kept fighting. He raped me. It was the most terrible thing I've ever endured.

What a contrast to the way love is supposed to be! True love is first true friendship. True friendship (which obeys God's moral laws) in a guy-girl friendship brings so much absolute joy. Real friendship never gets tired of waiting.

**Love (real friendship) is kind.** It always does things to and for the person that produce long-term positive and happy results in that person.

Ken Poure, a friend of mine from the West Coast, knows a lot about love and friendship. A few years ago his 16-year-old son came to him for advice before his first car date. He was really excited — first date!... beautiful girl!... the car!

To this boy, whom he loved so much, Ken began to ask some loaded questions.

"Are you planning on marrying this girl?"

"Aw, no, Dad, it's just our first date! I haven't even thought about marriage."

"That's okay — only about one out of a thousand early dating relationships becomes a marriage. Let me ask you another question."

"Fire away."

"Do you suppose your date will marry some guy someday?"

"Sure, Dad, she probably will. She's a great girl."

"Can I ask you another question?"

"You bet."

"Do you think *you* will marry a special girl someday?"

"Oh yes, I plan on it."

"Do you think your future wife is out there in the world somewhere tonight, looking forward to meeting you someday?"

"I sure hope so!"

Ken looked his son squarely in the eyes. "Do you suppose that girl — your future wife — is having a date *tonight* with another boy?"

After a long pause, his son answered, "I think she just might be going out right now."

"How do you want that boy to treat her tonight?"

"Dad," he said, looking up quickly, "if he lays one hand on her I'll kill him!"

"Then you treat your date the same way you want that boy to treat your future wife, and you won't have any problems."

Love is *kind.* Another true story paves the way to understanding this key to friendship that produces long-term happiness:

John had just been involved in a sexual relationship and had lost fellowship with the Lord. After getting his life together, he decided to respect girls more highly and not do things he would later regret.

After a few months he met Leslie, a neat Christian girl. They began dating — doing fun things together like playing miniature golf, go-cart riding, playing tennis, and so on. Though they dated for months, they never became physically involved with each other. Mark, John's roommate in college, kidded him constantly about this "abnormality." But John upheld his respect for Leslie and his own commitment to the Lord.

Sometime later, John and Leslie broke off their dating relationship. Soon afterward, Mark began going out with Leslie, and they eventually were married. At the wedding John looked Mark in the eye and said, "Now, aren't you glad I never kissed her?"

If you could look on the flip side of kindness, it would read, "Love isn't cruel — love doesn't make your friend hurt." So please don't tell your boyfriend you love him if you're only playing with your sex to try to win his love...and don't tell your girlfriend you love her if you're only playing with your "love" to try to win her sex. That's really not kindness at all...as the following letter shows.

*Since I started dating I have always promised myself that I would stay a virgin until I was married. I have lived to that promise until the past year. He said that he loved me and like all of the others, we would get married.*

I really believed that he loved me. After our first time, I started taking the pill to keep from getting pregnant. Two months later he dropped me for his old girlfriend (who was once pregnant by him). I felt as if I had 200 knives go through me. I was crushed.

Another girl wrote me the following regretful letter after a lot of "friends" advised her that sexual friendships were fun and rewarding.

The thing I regret most in my life would have to be losing my virginity. I was so young and most people don't think twelve year olds (7th grade) even know about sex. But I did and he did. We really didn't think it was all that wrong. I got my first kiss and lost my virginity all the same day! Then I met a guy at a football game from the other team. We left early from the game and went to the lake. I had only known the guy for less than an hour and have never talked to him since. I'm sure I was the talk of the bus on the way home for them. Then I started dating a wild guy. I made the first date so I could prove to him I would go to bed with him. That relationship lasted for about two months. He found another girl. They are now broken up. It took seeing my best friend who I had grown up with run away from home, O.D., and finally go through an abortion before I realized what I was doing to myself. She sees a shrink three times a week. And you still cannot carry on a normal conversation with her. I used to cry myself to sleep at night over all the things that I had done.

**Love (real friendship) does not demand its own way.** A real friend will never say, "If you don't drink this or take this or smoke this or put out sexually, then I'll look down on you or quit being your friend." That demanding attitude often works both ways in a relationship. The results are costly.

About a year and a half ago, I started dating a guy - just for fun. My parents did not approve of the relationship and they wanted me to break off with him. However, I did not listen to them but continued to see him. After four months we started having sex.

We had just pushed each other too far with petting and teasing. My weakness and sin in that one area of my life caused me to be weak in other areas... I began to party with friends and on occasion I was unfaithful to my boyfriend. This past spring I was still dating that one guy. I had been dating him for over a year and I really loved him. I know he also loved me but we kept disagreeing and breaking up. In April I discovered I was pregnant.

My boyfriend and I were very worried and when I had a test and the pregnancy was confirmed, we became frightened. The weekend before I was scheduled to have the abortion, my boyfriend and I broke up. I went out that night and got drunk with another guy. The next night I snuck out of my house to be with this guy and was caught by my parents. The night after that I went out again, this time with another guy and got into trouble again with my parents. I was trying to run away from my thoughts. I had the abortion. It was the most traumatic experience of my life. No one was there for me.

**Love (real friendship) does not rejoice in unrighteousness.** Friends don't give you bad advice or make you feel good about making the wrong decisions. Hurting a friend or getting messed up with a friend is not a party. A 16-year-old Kansas girl describes it vividly:

You're always telling us kids that premarital sex isn't love, but if it isn't why does it make me feel loved and secure with someone?

Read on, as she answers her own question:

You see, I don't base my relationship with my boyfriend on sex, because I still do it with an old boyfriend. He says that we're good friends and that it's alright because he loves me. I'm not proud that all this happens, I wish it didn't.

I received that letter in March. In April she found out she was pregnant. In May she had an abortion. In July I spent hours with her trying to put her shattered life back together again.

*"He told me he loved me..."* That's what they say. But love does not rejoice in unrighteousness.

One weekend I was in Dallas visiting a friend of mine. She and I always said that we would never 'go all the way' with a guy until we were married. Well, she was dating an older guy also and had given up her virginity. She told me how she thought it was the right thing to do now. I began thinking about it because over the past few weeks Rich had been suggesting that we should. Previously, I would always say no right when the point was discussed. Well, that night she and Curtis and Rich and I all went out. We went to Curtis' frat party and got pretty wasted. Since my defenses were low, and morals were shifting in the wrong direction, I submitted to the desire. It really made me feel like I was important (however, it was only pointing me in the wrong direction). Since we didn't have Christ in the center of our relationship, and I listened to my friend's advice I made the worst decision of my life.

Why was I so stupid?

You'll find a lot of "peer advice" today to support any questioning of biblical values about how our loving Creator made us to be our happiest. Every moral law He established is under fire today — even such "abominations" (things God hates) as men having sexual relationships with men and women having sexual relationships with women.

A gay college student I met a few years ago wrote me this letter after he had run with a homosexual crowd for several years:

Gay is not good nor is it a happy way to live. The very people who claimed they were happy where they were at, on a deeper level of communication admitted they were miserable and had the lowest self-esteem later on. These people who claimed they were happy being gay were actually more miserable than the people who said they were miserable being gay! I talked to well over 200 individuals and there were no exceptions to this. I myself fit into both categories at one time or another. Any homosexual - even if he doesn't admit it to anyone but himself - wishes that he were something other than what he has let himself become.

Love does not rejoice in unrighteousness. Another way to phrase this quality of friendship would be to say, "If you're my real friend, you'll never ask me to do anything that is wrong in God's eyes."

The following letter underlines the reality of what happens when this test of love is broken.

THERE WAS ONE BOY WHO REALLY SEEMED TO LIKE ME. HE WAS DEFINITELY THE

'RIGHT' TYPE; HE BELONGED TO THE RIGHT CLUBS AT SCHOOL, HE WAS IN THE RIGHT GROUP, HE WAS VERY CUTE, A GREAT ATHLETE, ETC. HE WAS THE PERFECT KIND OF GUY AND MOST IMPORTANTLY, HE LIKED ME. IT WASN'T AS IF I HAD LIKED HIM FIRST. I DIDN'T. HE MADE ALL THE MOVES TO SHOW ME THAT HE LIKED ME, HE WOULD SIT BY ME AT LUNCH, CARRY MY BOOKS FOR ME, CALL ME EVERY NIGHT, ETC. I LOVED IT! NOBODY HAD EVER PAID THAT MUCH ATTENTION TO ME BEFORE. IF ONLY I HAD SOMEONE TO TELL ME WHAT HE REALLY WAS, A TOTAL FLIRT, A SELFISH CHARMER, TWO-FACED, TRYING TO MADE HIMSELF LOOK BETTER—THE LIST COULD GO ON AND ON FOREVER. FOR ME, HE WAS A WOLF IN SHEEP'S CLOTHING. MY BIGGEST MISTAKE WAS LISTENING TO HIM IN THE FIRST PLACE. HE WOULD SAY 'I LOVE YOU' OVER THE PHONE, NOT THAT I BELIEVED HIM, BUT I ALWAYS FELT OBLIGATED TO SAY SOMETHING BACK. AT FOOTBALL GAMES WE WOULD TAKE 'WALKS' AND HE WOULD PRESSURE ME INTO DOING THINGS THAT I DIDN'T REALLY WANT TO DO. EVERY TIME I HAD A CHANCE TO SAY NO, THERE WAS AL-

WAYS A STRUGGLE IN MY MIND. THE MAIN REASON I WENT AHEAD WITH THE RELATIONSHIP, I THINK NOW, WAS TO PROVE TO MYSELF (AND MAYBE OTHERS) THAT I COULD HANDLE IT. I DIDN'T REALIZE THAT GOD WOULD PUT ME INTO A TRUE LOVE RELATIONSHIP UNTIL I WAS READY. I SHOULDN'T HAVE RUSHED MYSELF. I REGRET MY ENTIRE RELATIONSHIP WITH THAT BOY, IT WILL ALWAYS BE ON MY MIND. IT IS STILL HARD FOR ME TO BELIEVE HOW JUST ONE NIGHT COULD AFFECT MY LIFE SO GREATLY. THROUGH THE EXPERIENCE, THE LORD HAS TAUGHT ME TO LOOK TO HIM BEFORE I MAKE ANY DECISION. HE TAUGHT ME TO WAIT FOR HIS WILL BEFORE JUMPING INTO ANYTHING. HE ALSO TAUGHT ME TO RESERVE MY LOVE FOR THAT ONE SPECIAL MAN THAT GOD HAS PLANNED FOR ME.

**Love (real friendship) rejoices in the truth.** Love causes you to be excited when your friend makes a decision to live God's way — in a way that God says will make us truly fulfilled.

Someone said to me last summer, "I bet all you get are sad letters from people with problems." I answered, "No way!" I get many happy letters too:

Before I started coming to camp three years ago. I thought it would be okay to sleep with a guy if I had been going with him for a while. But since I've come to camp I've changed my mind. I feel that the greatest gift I can give the man I'm going to spend eternity with is my virginity.

A college freshman wrote this to me:

Joe, here's why I've decided to protect my virginity. Trust is one factor. Do you want that guy or girl to always believe you? If you are dating and you already have had sex with that person, how is he or she going to know that you didn't with someone else? Even after marriage if you're too friendly with the opposite sex it causes them to have feelings that aren't always Christlike, simply because they are afraid that you might have an affair. In this world today it is a fight to stay a virgin. Not just because of the peer pressure that 'everybody else is doing it' but the simple fact that you feel like you really love that person. My solution to the really love that person problem is this; if you really love that person you would want the best for them and would always want to be giving your best as Christ was. What could possibly be the best gift you could give your future wife or husband? It would be if you could honestly say to that guy or girl on your honeymoon, 'I have never been touched before, no other man or woman has ever had this gift I am about to give to you.' Your reward will not only come from God but from the joy you will see in their eyes and heart; for that person can walk along the street and know that they are the only person to have touched you. There will be no shame.

**Attach these qualities** of true friendship together and God's beautiful (and intensely practical) description of love sounds like this:

> Love is patient, love is kind, and is not jealous; love does not brag and is not arrogant, does not act unbecomingly; it does not seek its own, is not provoked, does not take into account a wrong suffered, does not rejoice in unrighteousness, but rejoices with the truth; bears all things, believes all

> things, hopes all things, endures all things. Love never fails... (1 Corinthians 13:4-8)

I really like *The Living Bible* paraphrased version of those same verses:

> Love is very patient and kind, never jealous or envious, never boastful or proud, never haughty or selfish or rude. Love does not demand its own way. It is not irritable or touchy. It does not hold grudges and will hardly even notice when others do it wrong. It is never glad about injustice, but rejoices whenever truth wins out. If you love someone you will be loyal to him no matter what the cost. You will always believe in him, always expect the best of him, and always stand your ground in defending him....love goes on forever.

In guy-girl relationships where real friendship isn't happening, it often seems that it's always the guy who is defrauding the girl and lying to her about love. But after studying the Bible carefully and talking to thousands of guys and girls with friendship problems, I really do believe that it usually takes two people to make a tragic mistake in a "friendship." A letter from a girl who is a college junior underlines this truth.

My dating was constant—constantly changing. I wasn't looking for a companion but a conquest. I found married man a real challenge—to see how much it would take before a man would cheat on his wife.

Girls need to realize that they have an important responsibility in the relationship too! A girl helps a guy remain pure in his thoughts and actions by:

① Not "teasing" him with suggestive clothes, playful hands, suggestive statements, passionate kisses, etc. These things are almost impossible for most guys to handle.

② Saying no when he's having problems drawing the line. It's the best favor you can do for him in that situation. And the sooner you say no, the better.

③ Remembering that *respect* is the main quality guys are looking for in a girlfriend they can REALLY love.

A 17-year-old girl wrote me while going through a frustrating dating relationship. "Joe," she said, "all I want is for him to treat me like his little princess." My advice to her was the same as it would be to you. If you want to be treated with respect like a princess, then begin to live like a princess — with respect for yourself and for others. □

1
NOW
2
IN A WHILE
3
worth waiting for...

Chapter 6

# LET'S MAKE A DEAL

What do you really want?

Whenever you desire something, the first critical step toward finding it is deciding exactly what it is you want, and how badly you want it.

So what do you really want in your relationships? Is it happiness and real friendship?

Play a crazy little game with me for a minute, and I can help you begin to find your rainbow. Pretend you're in Hollywood appearing on a TV game show. You've just won a thousand dollars, and you are standing beside the program host.

You're nervous. You're excited. And now you've just made the awesome decision to trade in that thousand dollars and go for the big prize of the day. This is an opportunity you'll never have again!

In front of you are three oversized doors, and behind one of them is the prize you must choose. The announcer turns to you and says, "Let's see what's behind Door Number One!" His pretty assistant smiles and waves her hand. The first big door opens...and there, yours for the choosing, is a double-dipped Baskin & Robbins ice cream cone (the flavor of your choice). It does look good. But you quickly remember you just gave up a thousand dollars, so you ask the announcer for a look behind Door Number Two.

As it opens, you nearly faint. What you see is a shiny new red Camaro loaded with every accessory. It's really a beauty. Just as you start to say, "I'll take it," the announcer says to his assistant, "What does that tag say?" She takes a card from the windshield and reads, "Yours on your 21st birthday."

*Twenty-first birthday,* you think — *that's a few years from now.* "Let's see what's behind Door Number Three," you say.

The last door opens, and this time you literally fall into the announcer's arms. You are staring into the headlights of a $75,000 Ferrari. Unbelievable! You have always dreamed of someday owning one, and here it is!

But your heart skips a beat as you suddenly catch sight of a card on the windshield. "What does the tag on this one say?" the announcer asks his assistant.

"Yours to claim on your 24th birthday," she reads.

*So long to wait!* you think.

The announcer interrupts your inward groaning to ask, "Which prize will you take?"

What a decision! The ice cream now, the Camaro in a few years, or the Ferrari after a wait that's three years longer. Wow, what a hard one!

**Before you decide**, let me tell you a little about these three prizes.

The ice cream will taste delicious but it will last for only a few minutes. The thrill is gone as you lick the last drop of chocolate off your lips.

The Camaro is quite a car. For a few years you'll be quite flashy and you'll enjoy one of the best cars on the road, until it becomes out of date and joins the rest of its Camaro friends on the used car lot.

The Ferrari, on the other hand, gets better every day you drive it. A friend of mine has one, and says it gets more enjoyable and valuable every year. It's worth more today than the day he bought it years ago.

I told you this was a crazy game we were playing — but actually it is no game. TODAY you are standing before a big stage with three doors, and you're about to make the greatest decision of your life.

Instead of a $1,000 risk to see the three doors, you have something worth more than billions of dollars, something no amount of bucks can buy: the health of your mind, your body, and your soul, the only mind, body, and soul you have. The decisions you make as you play this "game" will literally be with you for eternity.

Door Number One and the ice cream cone represent easy, quick, cheap thrills and "one-night stands." You get high with a "friend" or have sex with a "friend," and then move on to someone else. The next day the thrill is gone. Guilt, hangover, addiction, and sorrow are all that remain. Many teenagers who take Door Number One never even see the other two doors.

Door Number Two represents a "friendship" that lasts a few months or maybe even a couple of years. You have to wait a while for these, and you have to invest yourself to have one. I remember a teammate of mine in high school who chose Door Number Two. Every Friday night for a whole year he split a case of beer with his "friend." They had a "blast" together. They got in fights, and wrecked some cars and their own lives, but they were loyal friends for that year. Every Saturday night he slept with his "girlfriend." If you had asked him then, he would have told you he was the happiest guy in school. But today he doesn't even know where those two "friends" live, much less how they are doing or how badly he hurt them. His "Camaro" lies wrecked in a ditch somewhere, but it was "fun" while it lasted.

Door Number Three is really something special, and many people today who choose the other two doors have no idea of the happiness to be found there. I've had the privilege (because of God's amazing grace) to know a lasting, meaningful relationship with my wife for seventeen years, and every day our friendship is more precious and more valuable than it was the day before. She is more beautiful, more lovable, more fun to be with than ever. I wouldn't trade Debbie Jo for all the money and all the cars and all the Playboy "playmates" in the world.

I've also been blessed with some true friends who would die for me if they had to. We've been friends for years, and I can honestly say I love them. We play sandlot football together, go hunting together, work together, laugh together, cry together. I can tell them *anything.* No, we don't push alcohol or drugs on each other. We respect each other far too much for that.

I've had the privilege of performing the wedding ceremony as some of my best friends were each married to the person who had become their lifetime bride. It's an indescribable moment when that beautiful angel comes down the aisle, and they stand toe to toe, look deeply into each other's eyes, and pledge themselves to each other for keeps:

> "I give you my life."
> "I'll love you until I die."
> "I'll stay by your side no matter what."

It's a moment of deepest joy that unfolds into a lifetime of pleasure, adventure, discovery, and satisfaction.

To choose Door Number Three is costly. It isn't easy to say no to yourself and pass up the first two doors, but that's what you have to do to choose the third one. I know it is hard to do sometimes. But again I'll ask the question I asked at the beginning of this chapter: What is it that you really want?

And remember — what you stand to lose or keep is your only mind, your only body, your only soul.

**I can recall one night years ago** as I put my four precious children to bed, and we began talking about heaven. They came up with some fantastic questions.

"Will we have to take naps in heaven?"

"Daddy, why is it that we'll never cry there?"

"How long is forever?"

"Will Mommy and Grandma and Pappy be there?"

"Daddy, will I know you there?"

"Will crippled kids still be in their wheelchairs?"

Heaven. It's the ultimate reward behind Door Number Three, the icing on the cake for the happiness you find now.

Jesus compared heaven to a great wedding feast, which in those days was the most exciting event in a community. As He continued trying to reach into our limited understanding to tell about something too wonderful to describe, He said the streets would be made of pure gold, so pure that it would be crystal clear. He said our home would be a "mansion." He said we would enjoy total love, without any broken hearts or sadness.

An older man I respect as much as any man I know told me that the slightest encounter with a friend in heaven will be more thrilling than the greatest intimate encounter here on earth.

It's well worth waiting for. But between the first two doors and Door Number Three there is a giant moral barrier, placed there by God himself. In Galatians 5:19-20 we read of the "deeds of the flesh," and included in the list are "immorality, impurity, sensuality,...drunkenness, carousings, and things like these." Then comes this sobering statement: "I have forewarned you that those who practice such things shall not inherit the kingdom of God."

Even in some so-called "Christian" groups, kids talk about how having sex is okay if you're "in love" or promised or engaged. All around me I see that lie, and to those who believe it, I see Door Number Three still closed.

Without the opportunity Jesus Christ gives a person to change his life, it would be impossible for many of us to face the future.

**Once again**, keep the scene in view: Before you, ready to reveal their gifts, are three doors.

And you can choose *only one.* □

Chapter 7

# First and Goal

No doubt about it — waiting for the best is really hard sometimes.

With peer pressure getting worse every year, with TV and music saying constantly it's okay to break all the moral barriers, and with our own basic desire for self-pleasure seeming to get in the way, it's a challenge to wait for Door Number Three.

But after searching hard for many years, I have found an almost magic idea that can give you the ability to go for the very best in your life.

Where would basketball be without the basket? What kind of game would baseball be without home plate? And can you imagine cheering for or playing a game of football that didn't have a goal line or goal posts? People would be running around in every direction, not knowing where to go. They'd have to change the name of the game to Demolition Derby or Footkill or Where-Ya-Goin' Ball. Whatever you called it, the game would get pretty ridiculous soon after the opening kickoff.

I'm convinced that most of our problems come our way because we don't have a goal to shoot for in our lives. Most teenagers and college students don't really know what they're living for. They're like a car driving in a desert without a map or compass.

The lack of a goal affects our relationships especially. Along comes someone with a proposition for a thrill, and off we go because we don't have a better idea for what to do with our lives.

A recent letter from a teenager shows what a lack of goals can do to your life.

I have lost all my goals in life. I wanted to be a doctor but I really don't Care. I've thought about running away. I need to escape. I've started drink-

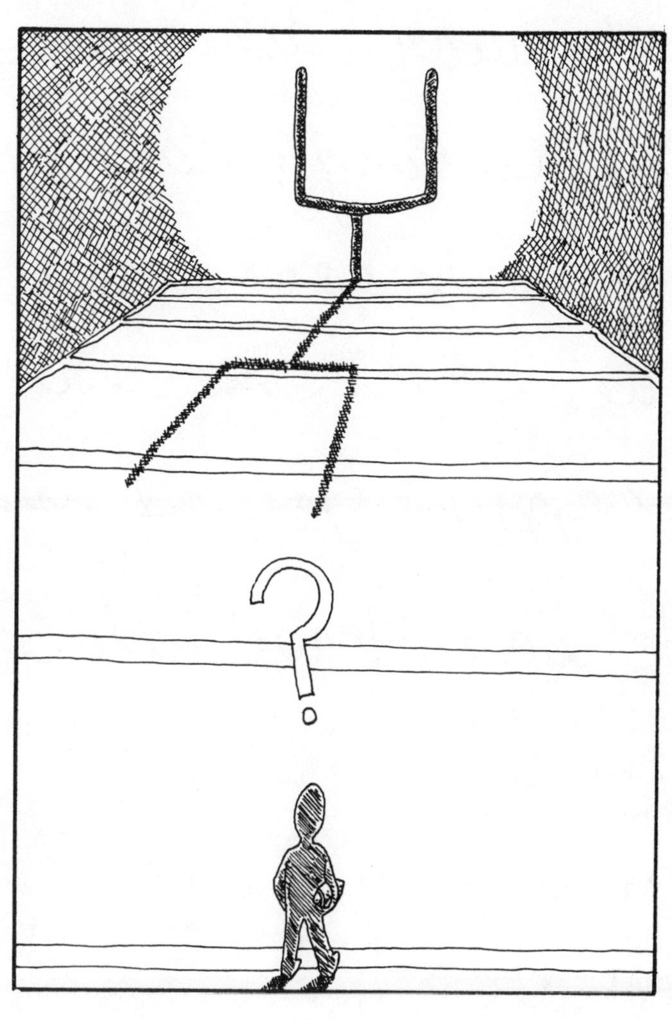

ing when my stomach aches for something; happiness, love, maybe God. I'm unhappy. Joe, I want to say forget this place and go get messed up and freak out.

Setting goals doesn't mean you have to decide what profession you're going to choose or who you're going to marry. It's simply setting a direction for the way you'll live.

Want to give it a try? (Watch out — it just might revolutionize your life!)

**First of all, decide** if you really want to live, or if you just want to exist like an amoeba until you die. Once you decide you really want to live, then make a commitment that you're going to go for the best with all your heart.

As you begin to set your goals, you need to follow a few guidelines if you want to be successful:

① You will be asked to set *Final Goals* for your life, and every other goal you set must agree with them.

② As you think about goals to pursue during a certain time of your life, select those that will help you lay a good foundation for achieving later goals — such as "Getting a good education" or "Having a happy marriage someday." For example, if you're now having problems with your sex life — and if you consider how guilt or having a venereal disease or going through a teenage pregnancy would hinder what you eventually want to do in life—then you may decide you need a goal of "Not having any sexual relationships before marriage".

③ Be really honest. This is not for anyone but you. It's your life. You get the payoff (good or bad) for how you live it.

With those guidelines in mind, let's go:

❶ **First, write down here your *Final Goals.*** Where and how do you want to spend eternity after you die? As you look back over your life on earth, what do you want to feel about it (pride, happiness, sense of accomplishment, relief, etc.)?

..................................................

..................................................

..................................................

..................................................

*(For some inspiring help, read Revelation 21:1-7 and John 17:3.)*

❷ **What are your *Marriage Goals?*** What kind of person do you want for a life mate? What do you want this person to be looking for in *you?*

..................................................

..................................................

..................................................

*(Read Proverbs 31:10 and 31:30, and 1 Peter 1:4-10.)*

❸ **What are your *Family Goals?*** What kind of parent do you want to be? What kind of husband or wife do you want to be? What do you want your family to be like?

..................................................

..................................................

..................................................

..................................................

*(Read Ephesians 6:1-4.)*

❹ **What are your *Career Goals?*** Not necessarily what job you want to have, but what kind of person do you want to be in your work? What kind of qualities do you want co-workers to see in you?

........................................................................................................

........................................................................................................

........................................................................................................

........................................................................................................

........................................................................................................

*(Read Colossians 3:23-24.)*

❺ **What are your *Retirement Goals?*** When you retire from your profession, how do you want to live your life?

........................................................................................................

........................................................................................................

........................................................................................................

........................................................................................................

*(Read Philippians 3:13-14.)*

❻ ***One-Year Goals:*** What are your goals for the coming year?

........................................................................................................

........................................................................................................

........................................................................................................

........................................................................................................

........................................................................................................

*(Read Proverbs 16:9.)*

❼ ***Immediate Goal:*** What is your goal for today? (Forever begins today — it's the first day of all that's left in your life.)

..........................................................................................

..........................................................................................

*(Read Proverbs 3:5-6.)*

**Now** — as the person responsible for the life you've just described above — sign here:

..........................................................................................

**These goals are yours.** You can look forward to a great and happy life if you'll keep your goals in front of you and not let yourself get sidetracked by something or someone who doesn't really want the best for you.

Here's how it helps:

I once received a letter from a single mom who was concerned about her teenager who was coming to our camp. She said her 15-year-old daughter was totally rebellious and unreachable. She also mentioned that a psychiatrist had said her daughter was "very disturbed," and that the daughter's high school coach said she was uncoachable.

After two weeks of camp I approached the girl and said, "Angie, how's your home life?"

"Pretty bad," she replied.

"How bad? Tell me about it."

She opened up and told me about her wild streak. I said, "Angie, how's your mom taking all of this? It's pretty hard raising a teenager without a husband, you know."

"Yes, I know. She's having a pretty rough time with me. But I'm not sure if I can change, or even want to."

"Angie," I went on, "do you hope to get married someday?"

"Sure."

"Do you suppose you might have a little girl someday?"

"I hope so! That would be nice."

"What kind of mother do you want to be?"

"A good one."

"How do you want your little girl to treat you when she's fifteen?"

"I hope she loves me and shows it."

"How would you feel if your 15-year-old treated you the way you're treating your mom?"

"Pretty bad, I guess." Angie dropped her head.

Lovingly I said, "Angie, that really doesn't make much sense, does it? What makes you think your little girl is going to treat her mom any differently than you're treating yours?"

A week after camp ended I got a letter from Angie. Here's how it began:

*Hi, it's me! You wouldn't believe the change since I've been home. My Mom and I are doing great. I'm even obeying her now. Pretty amazing, huh?*

Someday your goal for today may be to run away. Before you go, check out your future family goals. Are you going to learn on the streets how to work through problems that will arise in *your* future family — the family that you want to be one of the best? I don't think so!

Someday your goal for today might be to get "messed up and forget everything." Before you do, look over your goals for your marriage. If you want to find a life mate who is loyal and self-controlled and has class in everything he or she does — will what you do today help you become attractive to that kind of person? Or think of your career goals. If you want to be working with sharp, creative, productive, energetic people — will what you do today help you become the kind of person they would hire?

**Sometimes it hard** to think about those kinds of goals. In fact, your main motivation in life right now could very well be "to just be accepted by my friends." Acceptance is the most powerful driving force in the lives of teenagers today. As a friend of mine told me last night as we were driving across the state together, "Kids will do *anything* to be accepted by their peers. They'd rather die than be rejected."

I'll never forget the hurt I felt the first time I was rejected by my friends. I was a naive little pup in the fourth grade. I thought everyone was pretty much in love with everyone else. All my buddies were over at the home of a friend of mine who was mad at me for something, and I rode over on my bike. I still recall seeing all of them sitting around, drinking Cokes and watching TV. As I knocked on the door, one of them came over, locked it, and said, "Nobody's home."

"Nobody's home, what do you mean?"

"We just left, so scram."

Boy, was I crushed. Tears stung my eyes as I rode sadly away.

There were other times, too — like the night at a junior high school party when I asked this girl to dance with me. She looked into my eyes and calmly said, "No."

That will set you back a couple of years!

It's just plain hard to be rejected by your peers. But it is so much harder to become an addict or alcoholic or go through the misery of wondering every day if you got her pregnant!

Keep your goals fixed in the front of your mind

and don't betray yourself even when "friends" put you down for not joining in their wild ideas.

Here is probably the most honest and to-the-point letter I've ever received. It is written in the typical blunt manner of a 14-year-old boy.

Last night your talk meant a lot to me. I think I was on the wrong road, smoking pot every weekend and sometimes more just because of friends. Althought sometimes I did it because I wanted to, but when I did I felt all alone. I was even scared sometimes and smoking pot doesnt last for eternity, but Christ does.

Love,

Andy.

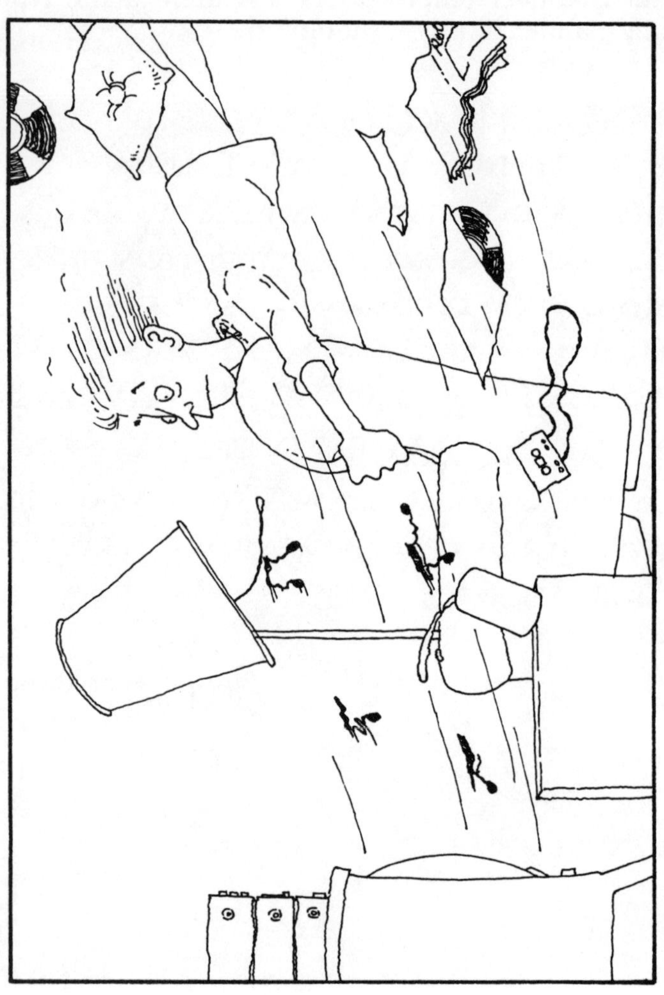

Chapter 8

# I WANNA HOLD YOUR HAND

As I would put my oldest daughter to bed at night during her younger years, when she was a bundle of giggles, dimples, Barbie dolls, tears, jack-in-the-box energy, pouting, ups, downs, blonde ponytails, and little-girl sensitive naive love — everything to make her Daddy's dream — I would often hear a familiar, "Daddy, hold my hand."

*Hold my hand* — isn't that also a picture of the friendship we all are craving? Everyone wants someone to trust with an almost childlike faith. Whether we hold that person's hand or not, we all long for someone whom we know will be there if we need help, someone who will never let us down.

The record charts shot off fireworks a few decades ago when the Beatles first hit America with a song expressing that friendship. "I Wanna Hold Your Hand" filled the radio airwaves for months, and sold more than ten million records.

As the nature of young friendships began to change drastically in the sixties, the seventies, and the eighties, so did the music of the Beatles and a thousand other rock groups.

Today the radio waves have mostly forgotten the sound of fulfilling expressions of true love (love that lasts forever), and of friendship that leads to holding another's hand (an expression of trust and commitment), and to smiles that come from happy, contented relationships. As the rock sounds of drugs, porno, punk, metal, new wave, and sex have escalated geometrically on the record charts, the drug addicts, teen alcoholics, unwanted pregnancies, and broken lives have mounted on the people charts.

Nothing has ever been any harder for me than writing this chapter. It will describe candidly the influences that undermine friendship today.

I know rock music is easy to get into and hard to turn off. It can make you feel relaxed, and help soothe your troubles (besides transforming your car into a four-speaker jam box). Of the hundreds of teenagers I've surveyed, 85 percent tell me they will listen to it no matter what the words are saying.

But much of today's music is frightening to a guy like me who loves kids, and who carries a broken heart over the subtle brainwash that is sending much of your generation into the junkyard of broken dreams and shattered lives. I responded with almost total disbelief as I began compiling the quotes and lyrics in this chapter for you to examine.

As I give you this evidence, I'll respect your intelligence and ability to see through what is merely my own personal opinion and prejudice. I find that kids today are ready for the facts, and they appreciate well-documented evidence.

I will not get into the issue of back-masking and the argument over the "beat" in music (although I respect the opinions and the evidence put forward by those who are concerned with those topics). This chapter will simply give an accurate survey of what musicians today are talking and singing about.

Scientific research on the brain continues to show

how similar the human brain is to a computer. The brain is "programmed" through nerve impulses received through your senses. It "thinks" whatever is fed to it through the ears and eyes, and through your senses of smell, taste, and touch. What goes in is what comes out. And it stores its information for a lifetime.

To put it simply, you are what you think; you become what you think about. In that sense you "create" your own personality and character by the input you give your "computer." You can stuff it with an arsenal of self-destructive missiles, or you can make it a storehouse full of supplies and tools to build an internal mansion of joy and strength and peace.

I can remember spending an hour one day with a young friend of mine at the local jail. He was on his way to the state penitentiary for his second hitch. Through a lot of painful sobs he said, "I just keep getting myself into trouble. I can't seem to make the right decisions." My mind recalled immediately the past years when this boy would always "turn off" the wisdom he heard, and "turn on" the pleasure, the lies, and the instant thrills. His mind was trained to tell him to do wrong.

I looked him in the eyes, and said (though it killed me to say it), "Mitch, it's time to pay up. You're going back to prison."

**You become what you think about.** Your personal "computer" has two basic components — the conscious, and the subconscious. They constantly interact and feed each other information.

Your subconscious is responsible for taking in and storing information that you don't "think" you're programming yourself with. The control our subconscious has over us is made evident by every cocaine addict who thought he "had it together" after his first joint, and every alcoholic who was "totally in control" after his first drink, and every murderer who was "just in a little fight" after his first outburst of anger, and every rapist who was "just having some fun" when he first sought out pornography.

Your subconscious is powerful. It stores trillions of "bites" of information — from the conversation and music we hear, from the books and magazines we read, and so on. It controls — actually controls — much of your actions.

You cannot control the thoughts that go from your ears and eyes into your subconscious mind. It is utterly impossible to watch a sex flick and then tell your mind, "Don't store that. It may cause me problems later."

A recent survey indicated that American teenagers listen each day to about two hours of a variety of popular rock music. That's about five thousand hours of listening from the ages of thirteen through nineteen — a lot of programming going into both the conscious and subconscious parts of your computer.

And what does that programming consist of? Let me share with you what your computer is being programmed to think, so you will know the source of the actions and attitudes that are growing inside you during these formative years of your personality.

The Grateful Dead crank the rhythm of their unsurpassed 190-speaker cabinet sound system. The band's most creative musician, Ron McKennan, died young from his storehouse accumulation of alcohol and drugs. Lead guitarist Jerry Garcia painted this picture of the source: *"Our lives are controlled by music."* The most popular book ever written (the Bible) gives agreement: "You become [are controlled by] what you think about" (Proverbs 23:7). Are you aware of what is gaining control over your life?

Detroit rock promoter Steve Glantz says much of the music of today's rock stars is "almost like Hitler-rock....That audience, because of the beat, is mesmerized by the music. They have that audience hypnotized. They could say, 'We're going out there and lift up this building,' and they'd just lift it up. That's the kind of *control* they have."

A few pages later I'll tell you the startling secret of who controls the songs that are gaining control over an entire generation. First, here's a brief summary of the information your brain is gaining as you tune into today's hits. (The information includes song lyrics as well as statements taken from articles in *Rolling Stone, Time, Circus Rock, Hit Parade, People, US,* and *Rock* magazines.)

### Category 1 — Sexual Perversion

As you think about this category and examine the evidence, keep in mind that millions of men and women are enjoying fulfillment and intimacy by following God's beautiful plan for the sexual relationship between husband and wife. The same can be true for your sex life. Without any perversion or fear or guilt, it can be your ultimate expression of God-given love to set your wife or husband apart from all other people in this world.

But check out the contrast in the message your "computer" is being fed from the most popular music ever recorded...

> Rock and roll is about sex...and I'm here to corrupt the youth of America.
>
> —Elvis Costello

> *Now I'm looking for a love that lasts;*
> *I need a shot and I, I need it fast;*
> *If I can't have her*
> *I'll take her and make her.*
>
> —Poison, "I Want Action"

> *I know this fat girl,*
> *She wears an orange skirt;*
> *You give her twenty dollars and she does her worth.*
>
> —L. L. Cool, "Bristol Hotel"

*The wetter the better;*
*Do it till we're black and blue....*
—Van Halen, "OU812"

*The blade of my knife that falls away from your heart*
*Those last few nights, it turned and sliced you apart....*

*Honey dripping from her pot;*
*Fill the cup to the top tonight;*
*This deadly sin is all we know...*
*Slide down to my knees*
*and taste my sword.*
—Motley C.R.U.E, "You're All I Need"
and "Tonight We Need a Lover"

I like strippers and wild parties with naked women. I'd love to own a whorehouse. What a wonderful way to make a living.

—Roger Taylor, Queen

*I'm a sex machine...*
*Get down, make love.*
—Freddie Mercury, Queen, "Don't Stop Me Now"

I'm on the job to exercise my sexual fantasies. When I'm on stage it's like doing it with 20,000 of your closest friends....I'm proud of the way we live....

I've managed to live out 100 percent of my fantasies with pretty women I've met on the road. We celebrate all the sex and violence of television.

—David Lee Roth

*I need a dirty woman.*
—Pink Floyd, "Young Lust"

A happy home life, security, and in-laws aren't conducive to making rock and roll.

—Rod Stewart

These statements and lyrics go a long way in explaining why forty percent of America's 19-year-old girls have been pregnant — with nearly half of those ending up in an abortion clinic.

Ted Nugent sings in "Jail Bait" about his craving for sex with a 13-year-old. Mick Jagger boasts of his desire for his daughter to have sex "at an early age." *Circus Rock* magazine calls Van Halen "a group of barbarians...sweeping around the world....And when it's done they have a barbarian party after each city is conquered. Van Halen says it this way: 'After it is over we go looking for women and children.' "

One magazine reports an account of the group Led Zeppelin dousing a rock prostitute with urine and perverting her sexual areas with "a certain animal."

Producer Bob Ezrin states that the group Kiss is "a symbol of unfettered evil and sensuality." His description is terribly accurate. Kiss member Gene Simmons boasts of having sex with more than a thousand women, and the group's song "Plaster Casters" is about rock prostitutes who make plaster replicas of rock stars' genitals.

The pages of this book could not contain all the examples of totally warped ideas about sex that are entering the minds of those who listen to this music today. The result is seen especially in the hundreds of thousands of rapes that occur annually in America. You just can't imagine what a tragedy it is until it has happened to a friend. (I've looked into those tearful eyes far too many times.)

Most respected psychologists agree that the cause for the rampant increase of this crime is the constant suggestion of abnormal sex from the mass media that surround us. For millions of young people, sex education begins with what they hear from their radios and stereos — and the effects are sometimes permanently destructive.

Again —

*You become what you think about;*
*You become what you see;*
*You become what you hear.*

### ➡ Category 2 — Sadomasochism: The Ultimate Perversion

Sadomasochism is the practice of brutally beating a sexual partner during the sexual encounter. I can't imagine the depravity of the mind that would tell a guy to tie up a girl and start beating, whipping, kicking, or biting her viciously while she gives you what God intended to be a priceless and precious wedding gift.

Again, music is propagating the perversion...

In "Tattooed Love Boys" Chrissie Hynde of the Pretenders tells of a girl who requires plastic surgery to mend the wounds inflicted by her lover. She sings of sex that "turns to anger" and a kiss that "turns into a slug."

In a *Rolling Stone* interview Judas Priest gives this boast: "To a certain extent sexually I have always been to the fullest extent in agreement with the experience sadomasochism has to offer." No wonder an ad proclaims, "Judas Priest has sin for sale."

Mick Jagger's view of women comes through vividly in songs like "When the Whip Comes Down" and "Am I Rough Enough?"

According to a *Rock* magazine interview with a Gene Simmons of Kiss, "cycles and whips" are "all the things little girls dream about." Consider the Kiss lyrics to "Bang-Bang You":

> *I'm gonna bang-bang you;*
> *I'll shoot you down with my love gun, baby...*
> *I'll be the villain in your book of dreams.*

Imagine how a girl feels when the party's over, and she's been abused by some self-seeking guy who wants to be the villain on every page in her book of dreams.

This complete lack of concern for a girl's heart comes screaming out in the Kiss song "Good Girl Gone Bad":

*She's a good girl gone bad;*
*One kiss can drive me mad.*
*She's out of control...but I'm having my fun.*

Equally perverse is Alice Cooper's "Cold Ethyl," a song about having sex with a dead woman's body:

*One thing's no lie;*
*Ethyl's frigid as an eskimo pie.*
*She's cool in bed;*
*She ought to be, cause Ethyl's dead.*

## Category 3 — Drugs

Rock music has been the number one public propagator of drugs in the past decade — with no regard for the countless deaths and the imprisoned lives (another teenage addiction every 45 seconds)...

Acid rock is music you listen to when you're high on acid.
—Jerry Garcia, the Grateful Dead

I can sing better after shooting smack (heroin) in both arms than after eating too much.
—Linda Rondstadt

*Chop your breakfast [cocaine] on a mirror;*
*Try me and you will see*
*More is all you need.*
*Dedicated to how I'm killing you.*

—Metallica

*Mr. Brown's store I used to do a little [heroin],*
*But a little won't do it—so the little*
*Got more and more.*

—Guns 'N' Roses

I'm in the music business for the sex and narcotics.
—Glenn Fry, the Eagles

> We avoid all hard drugs like cocaine although we do smoke marijuana now and again.
>
> —the BeeGees

> Shoot up heroin if you want to. It's your life. Do what you want to with it.
>
> —Motley Crue

I knew a pretty blonde girl who smoked pot and took an occasional trip on LSD. Then she gave birth to a baby who had only one arm. The doctors believed the birth defect was caused by a chromosome alteration from the mother's LSD.

The music makes it sound so good, and the musicians in their lifestyles try to back up the view. The reality of their stupidity, however, is seen in the mounting death toll among musicians. As their lies about drugs fill our parties, our cars and our homes, the musicians die in their own deception. Here are but a few names of those whose young lives were ended by drugs or alcohol or both: guitarist Michael Bloomfield; Led Zeppelin drummer John Bonham; Sid Vicious of the Sex Pistols; Bon Scott of AC/DC; Deep Purple's Tommy Bolin; Jim Morrison with the Doors (he screamed out in concert, "Cancel my subscription to the resurrection!"); Brian Jones of the Stones; Al Wilson of Canned Heat; Keith Moon of the Who; plus Jimi Hendricks, Janis Joplin, Vinnie Taylor, Shana Nalt, and more.

Their suicide path is behind the music that is selling the records. They want to take the listener with them to the grave. Consider these lyrics —

> *Forty thousand men and women every day*
> [the number of suicides annually],
> *You can find it today.*
> *You can be right here,*
> *C'mon, take my hand.*
>
> —Blue Oyster Cult, "Don't Fear the Reaper," from "Romeo and Juliet [teen suicide victims]—Forever in Eternity"

*Take a bottle and drown your sorrows—*
*A suicide solution.*

—from "The Suicide Solution" by Ozzie Osborne
(famous for his bloody, perverted concerts)

Also from Ozzie are these lines from "The Suicide Song":

*You're living a lie;*
*Such a shame—wonder why?*
*Why don't you just kill yourself*
*Cause you can't escape the master reaper.*

### Category 4 — The Occult

The occult movement is dedicated to the blasphemy of God and the Lord Jesus Christ. It appeals directly to Satan and his demons for power. Consider briefly the evidence of occult influence on today's music:

*I carry my crucifix*
*Under my deathlist,*
*Forward my mail to me in hell.*

*Our father*
*Who ain't in heaven*
*Be thy name on the wild side.*

*Take a ride on the wild side,*
*Wild side.*

—Motley Crue, "Wild Side"

*I believe in the devil,*
*I believe in the devil's child.*

—Judas Priest, "Devil's Child"

If there's a God in heaven, what's he waiting for? He leads his lambs to the slaughter house, not to the promised land.

—Elton John

*Ain't nothin' I'd rather do,*
*Goin' down, it's party time.*
*My friends are going to be there, too.*
*I'm on the highway to hell.*
—AC/DC, "Highway to Hell"

*Now I have you under my power;*
*Our love grows stronger now with every hour.*
*Look into my eyes,*
*You'll see who I am.*
*My name is Lucifer;*
*Please take my hand.*
—Black Sabbath, "N.I.B. — Nativity in Black"

In the album "Bat Out of Hell," the group Meat Loaf pictures demons and tells of a man who rides a bike out of Hades. The group's lead singer says, "When I go on stage I get possessed."

Jimmy Page of Led Zeppelin operates an occult bookstore in England called Equinox, and he lives in the mansion of Alexander Crowley, who renamed himself "The Beast — 666." One of the group's album covers shows nude, helpless children climbing a sacrificial altar, as well as a man holding up a child to Satan's sacrifice.

In "Hotel California," the Eagles sing vividly of the first church of Satan in San Francisco. The album cover features a picture of the church and its founder.

Alice Cooper, who sings "Welcome to My Nightmare," claims openly to be a reincarnation of a 17th-century witch.

The group Styx displays numerous Satanic symbols on their clothing and album covers. The group's name is from ancient mythology, in which the River Styx was the stream surrounding hell.

In the song "Sheep," Pink Floyd joins the other musical seducers in trying to get you to believe God isn't good, and that Satan is nothing to be feared:

*The Lord is my shepherd,*
*I shall not want...*
*He makes me hang on hooks in high places,*
*He converts me to lamb cutlets.*
*So we shall rise up*
*And make the bugger's eyes water.*

"Bugger" is a slang term for a homosexual pervert. Imagine a song reaching millions of teenagers in America that calls God a pervert, and implies that He will cut His children to pieces!

The list goes on and on.

### The Ultimate Rip-Off

*Big warm teardrops fell on my shoulders as I held my tender-hearted, 13-year-old daughter in a rare moment of deep sorrow —*

*"They got Babe," she sobbed.*

*Three handsome raccoons had invaded Jamie's pet fowl cage during the night and slaughtered her Canadian geese, as well as a Bantam rooster who literally had hatched in the palm of her hand a few months before. As one of those special people who know how to get intimately close to pets, she had hand-fed those precious feathered friends daily.*

*I felt like getting a shotgun and wasting the guilty critters, but Jamie cried, "No, Daddy, don't hurt the raccoons."*

Backstage, the electric-guitar-swinging-monsters slaughter young girls like cattle (while mothers cry — they know that their daughters, though enamored by the moment, will someday weep bitter tears).

Those who are victimized in backstage orgies are only a few compared to the thousands who are demoralized in the concert halls, and who so soon have the gift of virginity stolen from them. Put the same perverted sexual philosophy on radio and MTV, and six million good teenage girls every day take another step toward "A Good Girl Gone Bad." The results fill America's abortion clinics and psych wards and mental hospitals. The years go by, and the divorce courts become the scene for the ongoing teenage horror stories.

*"They killed Babe today."*

Does anyone care?

She's my little girl. I care.

Someday you will too.

### Make Your Move

God speaks very soberly to me, to the musicians, and to you. Please love yourself enough to listen to Him before it is too late.

> They proudly boast about their sins and conquests, and using their lusts as their bait, they lure back into sin those who have just escaped from such wicked living. "You aren't saved by doing good," they say, "so you might as well be bad. Do what you like; be free." (2 Peter 2:18-19, *The Living Bible*)

God is warning that the sinful music, the drugs, the sex, and the booze — all this that looks like a good escape becomes the master that enslaves the user.

Ask anyone how hard it is to give up his tapes when he knows how bad they are. Ask a pot smoker or alcoholic or sex addict how hard it is to quit. I've talked to many. They cry when they realize their slavery.

Let God set you free, my friend, before slavery becomes eternal destruction...

> But cowards who turn back from following Me, and those who are unfaithful to Me, and the corrupt, and murderers, and the immoral, and those conversing with demons, and idol worshipers, and all liars — their

doom is in the Lake that burns with fire and sulphur. This is the Second Death. (Revelation 21:8, *The Living Bible*)

Years ago, after Bon Scott of AC/DC died while choking from his all-day drinking binge, his group sang the hit "Hell's Bells" at his funeral, and chanted,

*I'm gonna getcha,*
*Satan's got Hell's bells....*
*If God's on the left, I'm on the right.*
*If you're into evil, you're a friend of mine.*

The most important choices you'll ever make are who you choose to be your friends. You can choose to follow Jesus and to be friends with others who follow Him, or you can choose his arch-enemy, Satan, the great deceiver. You cannot stand in the middle. "No servant can serve two masters, for either he will hate the one and love the other, or else he will hold to one and despise the other" (Luke 16:13, NASB). Let these words of Jesus motivate you to make a move today with your music, your movies, your television shows, and your friends.

"Choose for yourselves *today* whom you will serve" (Joshua 24:15, NASB). □

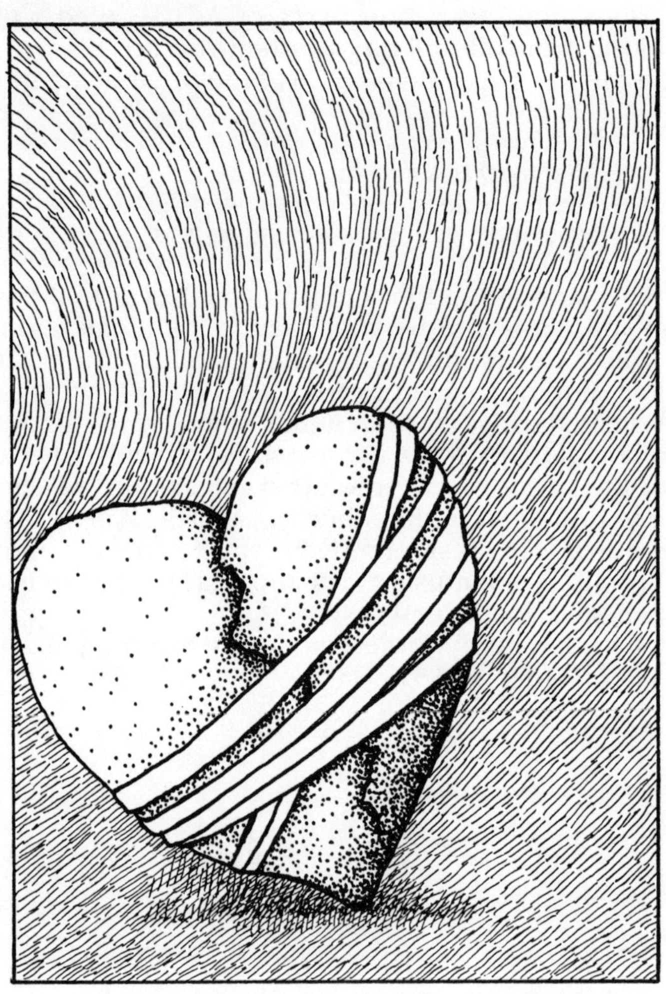

Chapter 9

# THE FRIENDSHIP CONNECTION

Do you remember, when you were a little kid, how much fun it was to save a dime and go get a box of Cracker Jacks all for yourself? I loved those gooey little things. The third best part was the popcorn, the second best part was the peanuts, and the very best part was...that's right...the surprise!

When I got engaged to my little honey, I hid her diamond ring in a Cracker Jacks surprise envelope, burying it deep in the caramel corn and peanuts. I carefully resealed the box wrapper to keep it from looking tampered with. I pictured the look of surprise she would have.

We drove to the top of a three-hundred-foot cliff overlooking a vast Ozark lake...a Kodak-perfect setting. The moment was rare. She opened the Cracker Jacks and took a bite...then sputtered. It tasted like the odorous rubber cement I had used to reseal the package. She tossed the box over the cliff.

I caught it just as it left her hand. "Wait!" I screamed. "What about the surprise? It won't be stale!"

Of course, when you're a kid you dig for the surprise as soon as you open the box. I used to wonder why they always put the surprise at the bottom. Even when you'd try to trick 'em and open the box from the bottom, the surprise would be at the other end. Anyway, it was still a lot of fun.

I am finding that friendship too comes in a special package. True friendship is very, very rewarding. It is better than you ever dreamed it could possibly be.

As a Christian I am really proud to tell you that my best and most loyal friend is Jesus Christ. A little story that happened to me years ago will help you understand why.

**One cold winter evening,** our daughter Jamie, who was eight, came home from gymnastics practice and mentioned that her best friend had made the "A" Team while she had been placed on the "B" Team. My wife, Debbie Jo — with her kind and sensitive heart — noticed Jamie's sad eyes and suggested I spend some "Daddy-Kid Time" with Jamie.

I took her in my arms and we sat in the rocking chair together, rocking for a long time (how we daddies love our little girls!). I told her how many times I had sat on the bench and didn't make the "A" team, and how God looks at our heart and not at what team we made.

After some stories and a lot of hugs, she felt better and ran off smiling. That night, as I tucked her into bed and kissed her good night, she wrapped her little arms around my neck and whispered into my ear, "Daddy, thanks for tying my heart back together."

"What do you mean, Peanut?"

"Well," she replied, "tonight my heart was broken bad, and you tied it back together again."

I too have had a broken heart that needed repair. I made some mistakes when I was a teenager. I knew I wasn't becoming the man I wanted to be. Then the best friend I had ever known walked out of my life forever. She had fallen in love with another "friend" of mine. I was so crushed, so heartbroken, that I cried every day for weeks.

There wasn't much left of me, but with what I had, I did the most important single thing I've ever done in my life. I said a simple prayer that has literally changed me one hundred percent. I looked up into the sky and said something like this: "God, I believe in You. I know You're up there somewhere and I know You love me anyway. I want to ask You, Jesus, into my heart today. I receive You as my Lord and Savior and personal Friend. Please forgive my mistakes. I turn from all of them. Jesus, I give my life to You."

HE CAME IN! Life for me began that day.

The first thing He did when He came into my life was tie my heart back together. It has been held together with love ever since.

Another thing He does when you invite Him into your heart is to wipe out all the sins you've ever committed. You need that! Everybody does. Guilt is the hardest thing on this planet to try to live with. *Only* Jesus can truly take it away. His perfect blood that poured out of His body when He was nailed up to that rough old piece of wood is the only thing precious enough to totally eliminate every imperfection a person has. You see, God hates sin so badly that yours and mine had to be washed out from the core with His perfect blood.

> As far as the east is from the west, so far has He removed our transgressions from us. (Psalm 103:12)

> For I will forgive their iniquity, and their sin I will remember no more. (Jeremiah 31:34)

I heard about the cross so much when I was growing up that I turned it off like a bad song on the radio. Then one day I understood the pain Jesus went through for <u>me</u>. He was beaten and tortured beyond description so that the beating *I* deserved would never take place.

I didn't listen until I understood that the spit Jesus took in the face that day represented all the filth and dirty thoughts and actions that you and I have committed in our lives.

I didn't want Him for a friend until I understood how hard it was for Him to be separated from His Father (God) for the first time ever — when He literally became a curse so that you and I would not be cursed and sent to hell.

I didn't want to love Him until I understood that it was love that kept Him on that cross for six hours of suffering. It wasn't three nails on a tree that kept Him there. He created those things! It wasn't the Roman soldiers that kept Him up there. He could have called in a tornado or earthquake or an entire universe of power to wipe out that band of men. LOVE kept Him on that cross. He stayed there for you. He stayed there for me.

I didn't think I needed Him until I realized He was all I had left. Now He's everything to me.

**The following letters** are some I've received in the last fourteen months from guys and girls like you, ages thirteen to twenty-five, who have asked Him into their hearts. Several of these letters are actually continuations of some of the sad letters from earlier pages in this book.

*You asked me if I had ever asked Christ into my life. And I hadn't, but we talked about it and that night I asked Christ to come into my life. Joe, I was so excited and happy. I was a different person and I* knew it. Well, Christ has stood next to me ever since then. And now I know that when I'm troubled and need a lift that I can turn to him and not pills. Life is wonderful and I wouldn't want to miss it for anything.

One of the most encouraging things to know about the Lord is that after you receive Him into your life, He will never leave you or forget you.

I was dating five different men. I began to feel guilty, I began to hurt, and I ran to a place where three years earlier I had run to -- church, and a pastor who cared. For two months that pastor talked to me practically every day about subjects ranging from the weather to moon walks, to God, to the men I was dating. He listened to me, gave advice (whether I took it or not was left to me—he didn't condemn me if I didn't). For two months he prayed for me and with me.

On Wednesday, January 5, 1983, I went to church and was drawn to five people. I watched them closely—there was something very different about them to me—they were so happy. At that minute some tight string inside of me broke and

I began to cry. I couldn't stop the tears, but I didn't want to—I was releasing something inside of me. Church ended and I went home. I remember sitting right smack in the middle of my bedroom floor crying out to God in desperation, in a last attempt before I ended my life. 'God, help me—I'm hurting—help me.' God heard me as I cried out to Him. He said, 'I want you back, no matter what you've done.'

As I sat there crying, I

felt a pair of arms go around me. I felt my head cradled to a shoulder- God picked me up that night and held me to His bosom. He whispered, 'Welcome home, I love you. I'm glad you're home, I love you. I've always loved you.'

God LOVES ME !!!!!

Jesus Christ has the desire and the ability to dig down deeply into your heart — so deep that He can change the desires you have had in the past.

There I was with a full bar in front of me, my favorite drinks and I had no desire to have a drink. It was neat to know that when my eyes are focused on Christ I don't desire unhealthy things. That made my night, little did they know that it is Christ who has been the source of my maturity. It is so encouraging to know that people do notice a change, even if they don't know the source of that change.

One of the most exciting things I've personally experienced and noticed others experience when they sincerely trust Christ with their lives and turn away from their sinful habits is the removal of the guilt problem. To some people it happens instantly. To others it takes years, but it does happen to those who are willing to walk (with Christ) away from their past.

When you talked to us about Cross-roads the other day, it really hit home for me. There was one particular phrase that you said about each of our faces and lives passing before Christ as He hung on the cross, that made me feel forgiven. I realized then that He accutally did die for each of us and and our sins; that no matter how terrible the sin, no matter how great the guilt, that I was forgiven. When I realized that He had already forgotten my sin, I cried for joy. It was like a weight that had been pushing down, crushing my heart had been lifted so that I could live life once again. It's such a beautiful feeling of true forgiveness. I am so overwhelmed with gratitude and love for Christ I can't believe it. With the abscence of guilt, I finally feel that I can look other Christians in the eye as if to say, 'Yes, I'm a sinner too, but I'm forgiven!

It's SO GREAT!!!

*I finally realized that the Cross-road is the road for me.*

*I intend to follow His "Road" the rest of my life. Not that I will be perfect but I will be forgiven.*

I watched our hometown team get romped in football last week. The finest athlete on the field played for the visitors. He was a 17-year-old friend of mine who played quarterback, defensive back and wide receiver. He had spent part of the summer at our camp until he realized he had a fairly serious disease. Eric expresses well how his relationship with Christ affects him even in the tough times:

*It's been another great year! I just wish that I could have been here for all of it, but like I've said before the time that I had off really brought me closer to Jesus Christ* than I've ever been before. And it was so neat, even though I was laying there, sort of down because of what all I was missing, just sort of talking to him, cause he's there as my best friend as well as my Saviour.

Every adult and teenager in this world loves to be free, to feel free, to live free. Without fail I've seen both good kids and troubled kids find this freedom when they turn to Jesus Christ with genuine commitment.

I had a couple of opportunities to go to parties last weekend, but I didn't. I finally didn't even desire to go at all.

It's neat the way God answers prayer. I finally said, "God, I can't handle this anymore, you gotta take over now!" It's so relieving now that it's gone. I would always try to give things to him, but I guess I keep trying to take them back. No way, now! It's too good to be free!

Here are four more letters that underline the reality of the fullness of life found in a personal friendship with Jesus Christ:

I did a lot of thinking about the two very different ways I have lived my life.

I have been so unhappy this past year and I have come to my senses and I've real-ized I want my old life back! I am so thankful to the Lord for never letting me go and for loving me no matter what I do and for always forgiving me! I am a new person, Joe, I am cleansed of every wrong I have ever done! That is the most wonderful feeling ever-Knowing that he is with me and I can trust in him completely! I am totally blown away by the fact that he gave his life for someone like me!

There have been times in my life when I have felt totally alone and that no one cared at all, but all along, helping me through the best and worst times of my life, there was Jesus! I am con-tinuing to grow in my relationship with the Lord and I am so excited about it that I just had to share it with someone.

□ □ □

I thank the Lord for letting me realize what it is like to be at the bottom and then shoot to the top. It's a feeling I can't describe... knowing I've got him there whenever I need him, not only that, but just all the time.

□ □ □

This was where my life turned around drastically. I accepted Christ into my heart and that emptiness that was once there was gone (I had something to live for again.) Now when I got back home my problems were still there but I had no desire to smoke pot or get drunk any more. Now even in my lowest moods he was there to be my friend and help me through my trials and tribulations. Jesus became my best friend even when I turned my eyes away from him he kept his eye on me.

□ □ □

But the most wonderful thing i've discovered this last month is Jesus Christ. Although I had been a Christian since I was a Child, I still had not devoted my life to Him as I have now.

WILL

Chapter 10

# WHO HAS YOUR WILL?

She was five-feet-one, and had long blonde hair and beautiful blue eyes. She really looked like the latest in dolls from an expensive toy store.

She also had a confused and broken heart.

I was interviewing university students to recruit summer staff for our youth camps when she came to my table. The more we talked, the more I realized that what she wanted wasn't a summer job. She wanted help.

Suzi had been involved in the wrong relationship for the past six months. She had trusted a friend who had taken advantage of her naiveness. The result was a torn-up 19-year-old.

After she had time to spill out to me a lot of sadness and guilt and emotion, we began to get to the heart of her dilemma. She had been a Christian since she was a little girl, but had "fallen away" from her faith when she was sixteen. She was so insecure because she thought all she had was her beauty, and felt that she needed to always use her beauty to attract men regardless of the consequences.

I told her about the love and acceptance I had seen so many young people find in Jesus Christ. I explained how He could tie back together her broken heart by forgiving all the mess that was behind her and giving her new life — a new Suzi who was beautiful not just on the surface, but inwardly, with a secure beauty that penetrated her entire personality.

She was fighting it. She didn't want to let go of her boyfriend even though the relationship was killing her. (Have you ever been there?)

I said, "Suzi, do you know what you need to do?"

Big tears ran mascara down her cheeks. "Not really," she answered.

"Suzi, there's one thing you've never given to Jesus."

"What is it?" she sobbed.

I said softly, "Suzi, you've never given Christ your will."

She looked up, surprised. After a pause, she said Will was her boyfriend's name — "And you're right — I can't give him up."

*That's pretty amazing,* I thought to myself. His name carried her problem in two ways. To her, Will was more important than happiness, forgiveness and real love. And her will (which is the part of our heart that controls what we do — the five-star general of our personality) didn't want to submit to Jesus Christ's will.

You can go to church forever and still never have a relationship with Christ. You can study the Bible, pray all kinds of prayers, walk the aisle of your church, get baptized, and do every religious thing imaginable, yet not know the assurance of your forgiveness, and the departure of your guilt, and the happiness of freedom in Christ.

Until you give Him your will (all of it) you'll not enjoy the Number One Friendship you could ever have in life — a hand-in-hand, fulfilling relationship with Jesus Christ through His Spirit, who is able to literally come inside *your* heart and live the moment you give your life to Him.

"But as many as received Him, to them He gave the right to become children of God" (John 1:12). Have you ever received Him as *your* personal Lord and Savior?

Jesus said, "Look! I have been standing at the door and I am constantly knocking. If anyone (man or woman) hears Me calling him and opens the door, I will come in and fellowship (be friends) with him and he with Me" (Revelation 3:20, *The Living Bible*).

It is your will that decides to open up your heart and let Him into your life. The single most important event in your life is the moment you give Him your will and say, "Lord, I can't do it alone. I need You to take my life. I give You my past. I give You my dating life. I give You my friends, my school life, and my family life. I give You everything. Lord Jesus, come into my life right now. Make me the person You want me to be. Thank You for forgiving me. I want You for my best friend forever."

Have you ever prayed that and meant it sincerely? If not, please read back over those sentences and put them into your own words. Let your eyes close as you communicate your desire and your decision to the living Christ...and receive Him into your heart today. □

Ed
Ed

Chapter 11

# A FRIEND NAMED ME

The halls outside the classrooms were empty. It was 6 P.M. Not far away, four hundred seniors were marching into the auditorium under the cover of those cumbersome caps and gowns. I was hurrying to be on time to speak to the graduation assembly, so I ducked into the school counselor's office to quickly slip on a coat and tie. As I charged out of the small room, a giant wall poster grabbed my attention:

DON'T GIVE UP YOUR SELF-RESPECT.

IT'S ALL YOU'VE GOT!

*Man,* I thought, *how totally true that is.*

What kind of a friend do you see when you look into the mirror? Can you honestly say you love yourself? Before you can be a real friend to someone else, you've got to be a real friend with yourself. And you can...oh, yes — YOU CAN!

No one has messed up so badly that he can't realize this great friendship. It begins when, as a true Christian, you view yourself in the same way as you are seen by your Lord — your God and your Creator.

God wants you to know His love so much that He sent His Son to die so there might be a pure, lasting friendship between you and Him. I've seen another poster on which someone asked Jesus, "How much do You love me?" In reply, He stretched out His arms as wide as He could — on the cross.

You are God's child when you sincerely trust Christ with your heart.

> But as many as received Him, to them He gave the right to become children of God, even to those who believed in His name. (John 1:12)

And because of what Christ has done, God sees His children as

PERFECT
LOVED
FORGIVEN
JUSTIFIED
ETERNAL
SECURE

In Hebrews 10:17 God says, "Their sins...I will remember no more." God loves you totally and completely. For God — who knows no time, and who has always been and always will be — still sees each of His children over the shoulder of the dying Christ on the cross. He still views the cross as painfully real — and His love for you will always be just as real.

Why do we have such a hard time remembering that? In our achievement-oriented society, we think we've got to earn everything. "Work hard in school and you'll succeed." "Work hard on the basketball court and you'll win." "Campaign hard and you'll be elected." "Work hard at relationships and they'll go fine." Work, work, work!

It's hard just to *accept* — without working for it —

the love God offers through Christ. But we simply cannot earn it. It is given freely.

> For by grace you have been saved through faith; and that not of yourselves, it is the gift of God; not as a result of works, that no one should boast. (Ephesians 2:8-9)

If you are a sincere follower of Christ, there's absolutely no way you can get God to love you any more than He does right now. He is one-hundred percent in love with you. Isn't that great to know!

As you've read this book you can probably tell how much I love my four children. Man, oh, man, this business of being a daddy is great! How much do you think I would take for Jamie, Corky, Brady, or Cooper? A thousand dollars? No way! A hundred thousand? Never! Ten million? Out of the question. A billion trillion dollars? NO! Each of my kids is absolutely more valuable than all the money that has ever been minted. I LOVE my kids!

Once when Corky was small I was carrying her up the road and I told her (for the thousandth time) how much I loved her. She cocked her little blonde head and looked into my eyes, and asked in her usual straightforward manner, "Daddy, do you love me as much as Jesus does?"

"Well, uh — hmm... No, Cork, I don't guess I do."

"Why?" Her eyes were open wide.

"I just can't. He loves you so much more than I do because I don't have the room inside of me for *that* much love."

Just think for a minute how much He must care for you. To Him, you were worth dying for. To Him, you have greater value than any diamond ever mined, any king who ever sat on a throne, or any star that ever shined in the sky.

Two things make it hard for us to accept that love. The first is false guilt that says, "What Christ did on the cross is okay for eternity, but it's not for me now. I don't deserve to be loved." The fact is,

God knows us better than we even know ourselves. One of the prayers of praise in the Bible tells about that knowledge:

> You made all the delicate, inner parts of my body, and knit them together in my mother's womb. Thank you for making me so wonderfully complex! It is amazing to think about. Your workmanship is marvelous — and how well I know it. You were there while I was being formed in utter seclusion! You saw me before I was born and scheduled each day of my life before I began to breathe. Every day was recorded in your book! How precious it is, Lord, to realize that you are thinking about me constantly! I can't even count how many times a day your thoughts turn towards me. And when I waken in the morning, you are still thinking of me! (Psalm 139:13-18, *The Living Bible*)

He knows us so intimately that He is completely aware of all our failings. Yet, for the very sins you and I commit, He sent His Son. Through the cross, He views you and me as perfect.

The second problem is the deception that says, "In order for me to be a good Christian, I am supposed to feel inferior and unimportant." But in God's eyes you are *SO* important! Did you know that if you had been the only person alive when Christ went to the cross, He still would have died for you? He loves you that much.

Many of us equate humility with low self-esteem. But humility is *not* inferiority. Humility is *not* underestimating our abilities. Humility is *not* self-hatred. Humility is knowing that only by God's amazing grace can you be the wonderful person He made you to be.

Our model and example of true humility is Jesus Christ Himself —

> who, although He existed in the form of God, did not regard equality with God a thing to be grasped, but emptied Himself, taking the form of a bond-servant, and being made in the likeness of men.

> And being found in appearance as a man, He humbled Himself by becoming obedient to the point of death, even death on a cross.
>
> Therefore also God highly exalted Him, and bestowed on Him the name which is above every name, that at the name of Jesus every knee should bow, of those who are in heaven, and on earth, and under the earth, and that every tongue should confess that Jesus Christ is Lord, to the glory of God the Father. (Philippians 2:6-11)

Experiencing this great love and acceptance from the King of kings and Lord of lords does make you feel good about yourself. The humility comes when you realize that He gets all the credit and without Him, you'd be back where you were before you knew Him. It becomes a give/give relationship that you'll enjoy forever: He gives you love, and you give Him the glory.

A 16-year-old who realized God's powerful love wrote me this:

I want to tell you how great it is to be a Christian. I was always skeptical of how true the Christ story was. Now I know He's real, I know He's alive and I know He's with me and the happiness is indescribable. It makes me feel good about me! Knowing that God loves us completely and unendingly is so reassuring. It does make us feel good about ourselves.

A17-year-old friend said this:

I became a Christian this summer; the most wonderful, special thing that could have happened to me. But before it wasn't like that. I hated myself. I ran away three times. During all this time I was just trying to survive. But now, thanks to Christ, I won't have to survive any longer. I stopped smoking and drinking and am looking forward to school and bringing my grades up. I can honestly say I like myself again, something I haven't felt in a long time.

As you wake up each morning realizing and thanking Him from down deep in your heart for all that you mean to Him, your road to being your own real friend begins. You can build up that road beautifully by consistently using <u>three essential tools</u>:

**First of all, focus your attention** and thoughts each day on what is really important to you. The world we live in will get you to believe (if you listen long enough) that all that matters is how you look or how you dress or how much in shape you are. But ask the Miss America who's grown old and wrinkled, or the ex-pro athlete who can't do anything but make beer commercials anymore, how important those things really are. God, however, gives us an inner beauty that external looks can't begin to equal.

**The second tool** is the truth that you build up your self-esteem by doing what you know you ought to do. That's why walking with Jesus Christ is so important! He gives you the inner conviction and strength to do what you know is right.

A 22-year-old single woman came by my house yesterday to seek advice. She had been living with a guy who had left her. She had done a lot of drugs and had totally run away from her mom's love and advice.

As we talked through the pages of her life, it was really sad to see what she had allowed herself to become — broken relationship after broken relationship, high after high, low after low. Her self-respect was just about gone.

As our conversation went on we began to see some real bright spots. She would smile, and her eyes would sparkle when she relived the times when she <u>had</u> said no to a temptation — times when she had stood strong on her convictions, when she had said yes to her mom's advice and yes to Christ. The self-respect she felt as she thought of those moments was there because she had been able to do what she knew she ought to do.

Starting today, make a determination to gain freedom and self-respect by making the right decisions and obeying God's guidance in your life. You'll be amazed how good it will make you feel.

**The third tool** that will build up the best part of you is to think about the good things you see in you, and quit beating yourself for the faults, the flaws, and the mistakes you've made. Yes, God has forgiven you, so now it is time to start forgiving yourself. Put the good things about you up on the bulletin board of your mind. Put up signs there that say things like these:

"God really *does* care for me!"
"I said no today."
"I'm getting better."
"I can do it!"

And take down the old dusty signs that say "I'm no good," "I'm unworthy," or "I can never forgive myself for that."

When you start to get down on yourself, just check out your bulletin board and smile as you look at all the good things you see.

For me personally, it works like this: My basic prayer each day is simple — "Lord, today help me take one small step closer to You, and keep me from stepping backwards." For all of us, growth often comes slowly — but we can fall back fast!

I can't take giant steps very well or lots of them at once, but I *can* take one step every day. The result is amazing! Every year I can look back on 365 small steps toward Him, and it's a difference I can feel good about.

The closer I get to Him, the easier it is to keep taking steps in His direction, growing in my love for Him. And I know that loving Him means loving me.

When I realize the price You paid,
the ultimate sacrifice You made
to prove to me the love You'd send,
then I can call You my best friend.

It's only, God, when I love You
that I can be my best friend too;
it's then I truly feel so good
and do the things I know I should.

Then those around me I can love
even though they push and shove;
it doesn't matter how they'll be
cause I'm secure when I love me.

Thank You, Lord, for loving me
and helping people like me see
that I can be my own best friend
and truly love myself again.

*— Joey Staples*

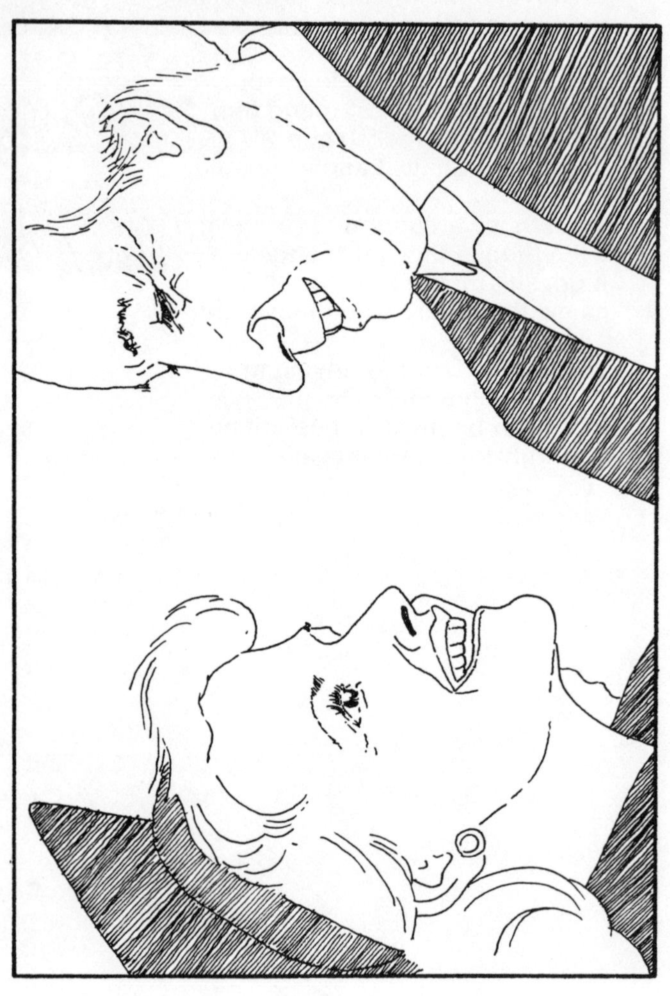

Chapter 12

# FAMILY FRIENDS

Second only in magnitude to your relationship with Christ is another special friendship, a friendship with potential most young people never realize.

I'm talking about a friendship with those two people who brought you into this world in the first place — the folks who changed your diaper ten thousand times, who cleaned up countless messes you made, and who have cried more tears of joy and sorrow over you than you'll ever know. Maybe you have only one of them, or perhaps some proud grandparents have taken over the role. Or maybe you're one of those specially fortunate people who were chosen and adopted by some Christ-loving parents.

We take our parents' love so much for granted that it is a crime. Not until you have (or adopt) children of your own will you begin to fully realize their love. But don't let that stop you from making the most of the opportunities you have now to discover these fulfilling friendships.

An extensive survey showed that 80 percent of the teenagers in America would still spend time with their teenage "friends" even if their parents disapproved. I lost count a long time ago of the brokenhearted teenagers I know who disregarded their parents' friendship and advice. They kept seeing a "friend" anyway until the bomb exploded and the parents' wise warning came true.

Angie lived in Kansas City. She fell for a handsome guy who was three years older than she was. He had some problems, but she thought he would change. Angie's dad tried to put an end to the relationship because he could see she was going to get hurt. But she would sneak out of the house to see the guy. Eventually she ran off with him and got married.

Eleven horrible months later, Angie was back home with a broken jaw — evidence of where the guy's anger had landed. Angie's dad was waiting to receive her into his arms and help her patch up her shattered life.

I remember spending some time with a high school junior who had just attempted suicide. I had known her earlier, so I eagerly anticipated our getting together. As we talked, she told me how bad things were at home. She said her parents didn't love her and were always comparing her to her sister. She had built up quite a hatred for her dad. She said she couldn't go on living that way.

As our conversation went on she began to discover that she was part of the solution to the problem. She had expected her parents to be perfect and felt it was their responsibility to do all the giving. We began to focus on all the good qualities in her dad. She was amazed as she came up with a list of more than twenty wonderful qualities she had been overlooking in her dad.

She made a commitment to begin to focus on these good things and forgive him for being imperfect and for having some weaknesses. (Fortunately, I had the opportunity to spend some meaningful time with her parents later that week to help them understand her better.)

A month later I got the following letter from her:

How are things in Branson for you? You would not believe how great things are here at home. I can't remember the last time things were so good with my parents and me. We're a family once again. I'm able to tell them that I love them and mean it and feel good about it. It's like I came home with the wrong family, but I know now that it's me. I'm different in my own ways, and I'm looking at my parents from a completely different perspective.

I want to thank you so much for spending the time with me and helping me see through the forest. I also thank you for your prayers and confidence in me. I know you're behind me all the way, but even better I have my best friend, Jesus Christ. I wouldn't be able to live without him. I love him so much and I know he loves me.

Wouldn't it have been a tragedy — as every suicide is — if this girl hadn't come to her senses and found her new perspective? Think of the happy years she would have missed.

I've talked to so many teenagers who have attempted — and, fortunately, failed — to end their lives. Not one wishes he or she would have succeeded. Every single one is so glad to still be alive.

Your problems will end. Daylight will come. You can find your parents' love again! You've got to give them a chance.

A 17-year-old tells a familiar story:

Now I still need to talk to you about my parents. I do obey them with somewhat of a smile. It's really hard though because I really don't feel much love for my parents. I mean sometimes I can't control my thoughts and feelings toward them. I wish I could get the feeling that I would love to do stuff for them. I have to go very much against my thoughts to do a job or favor for them. I guess I don't have the right kind of love for them. My family is going to a counselor right now because my Mom really does feel bad. I think I can really love my Mom, but it's very hard for me to be in the same room with my Dad.

Here are some practical things you can do now to find that exciting friendship right there in your own home:

**1. Thank your parents for everything they do for you, as it happens.** Try to thank them at least ten times every day. (You'd be surprised how easy it is to find ten things to thank them for — and if you're sharp, you can find a hundred!) If you're away in college, you can write them *today* a long letter full of thank you's for all they've done.

I learned one of the greatest lessons in my life about being thankful one day when my six-year-old daughter asked me to help her build a toy "wagon" out of wood blocks with hickory nuts for wheels. I was busy, but it seemed a neat opportunity to spend time with my Little Love Bug. We got the wagon about eighty percent done that afternoon, and took a break to let the glue dry. But I forgot to finish it for her.

That night as I headed for bed — dead-tired and ready to crash — I saw a little note taped on my closet door. In a six-year-old's print (different size letters, slanted lines, and the rest), it read:

> I love you, Daddy. Thanks for taking time to make my wagon. Love, Corky

I almost cried. After I showed my wife the note, I ran up to the shop, grabbed the little wagon, and worked tirelessly until it was done.

Because she took time to thank me for what little I <u>had</u> done, I wanted to finish it for her. The next morning it was waiting by her plate when she came to breakfast.

**2. Tell your parents often that you love them.**

Anne was fourteen. She came to me with a deep personal problem. To make a long story short, she told me how she had lost all her happiness — she said she just felt rotten all the time. After I had listened for quite a while, she said that she hadn't told her parents she loved them in three years. She knew they needed to hear it, but she found it very hard to tell them. After we talked more, she said she'd write them that day and let them know she loved them.

The next day she was all smiles. It was as if someone had lifted a hundred-ton weight off her back. "How could one thing so little make such a great change in me?" she said. "I feel like a different person inside." Maybe it wasn't as little a thing as she thought!

**3. Listen to your parents with an open mind.**

A 17-year-old paints a clear picture of the tremendous value of gaining your parents' wisdom in every area of your life:

*As I was growing up my parents always told me to stay away from drugs. I didn't know then that* alcohol is a drug too. I started drinking in 7th grade. It seemed like the thing to do. All my friends were doing it so I joined in the "fun". They looked like they were enjoying themselves. Soon after that I was laughing right along with them. I didn't understand that drunkenness is not a funny thing. Actually it is very sad. People don't realize at the time what they're getting into. I sure didn't. I never thought my life could end up like this. My life will never be the same and I owe it all to drugs.

About a year later I was introduced to marijuana. I always wondered what it was like and again, all the kids were doing it so I had to be "cool" and smoke pot with them. Now I wish I had listened to my parents. But when I was stoned everything seemed so peaceful and I thought nothing could hurt me. When something was bothering me, I would go out and get wasted and then I felt better. Little did I know that my problems were really getting worse because I wasn't facing up to them. Every time I got high I would say to myself, "Just one more time won't hurt But one more time led to many more times. It wasn't just a weekend anymore. By my sophomore year I was getting high daily. It was so easy to get and when someone offered it to me, it didn't even occur to me to turn it down. Everyone thought I was funny when I was stoned. That's the only way I could get attention.

Then my brother got me into something totally different—speed. He told me it was fun and it would make me happy. I needed it to keep awake in school. So along with drinking and smoking, I was now on speed too. At first I just experimented with it, but I liked it so I kept it up. Then it got to where all that stuff wasn't enough—I needed a better high. Just about anything you could imagine was available at school. Some guy sold me a hit of acid. I had no idea what it would do to me. I just remember going on the worst trip of my life. It's too strange to explain. A person has to be on it to really know what it's like. I tripped all that night and part of the next day. I thought it would never end. I remember thinking I was going to die. That's when I decided that LSD was not my thing and I would never try that again. But I was still into the other stuff and even worse.

My friends and I would smoke joints laced with PCP. Some friends—they wouldn't accept me for who I was—they only liked me if I would get high with them. I began to skip school, ignore curfews, and didn't obey my parents at all. I wouldn't listen to anyone. They were always on my case about something. I couldn't figure out why they didn't leave me alone and let me live my own life. I always thought I could handle it, but now I was deeper into it than the people who started me on it. I was totally alone. I had no real friends. I began to get so depressed I wanted to die. I thought no one cared what happened to me. So one night when life seemed hopeless, I actually did it - something I had been thinking about for a long time. I sat down in my room and took a razor blade to my wrist. It wasn't until blood was going all over the place that I knew I didn't want to die. My mother took me to the hospital and I spent a month there in the mental ward. It was the hardest month of my life. I knew it was time for a change but I didn't want to quit partying.

It wasn't until after I got out of the hospital that I realized that's not the way to live

I wasn't going to get anywhere in life. I always knew God was with me and would never let me go. I prayed all the time for him to save me from this nightmare. Now I have a purpose in life and I am living for the Lord. I have been off drugs for four months. It has been tough, but I'm really proud that I was able to give them up. Now I can really be happy. Many young people today are misled by drugs. I hate to see what they do to people. Drugs kill people and destroy lives. I was one of the lucky ones. Through a lot of help and a *lot of pain, I was able to kick the habit. Now I have real friends and I realize that people really did care all along. I thank God every day that I'm alive and I'm completely forgiven.*

**4. Obey your parents in everything.** Everything? Yes—everything that doesn't go against God's basic moral laws. The great, loving Creator who made you has made this clear: In order for you to be the best you can possibly be, you need to obey your parents.

After a youth group meeting one Sunday night several years ago, Todd came up to me and said, "I've got something neat to tell you. I joined a church today."

"Todd," I said, "that's great!"

"Well, I'm not so sure. There's a problem with it."

"What's that?"

"The church I joined is Presbyterian, and my mom is a Methodist, and she doesn't think I should have done it."

"What about your dad?"

"Well, he's Baptist, and he doesn't like it either."

"Hmmm, that's interesting," I said, silently praying for help. "Todd," I continued, "I think you may need to do something that's going to be pretty hard."

He looked puzzled. "What's that?"

"Apologize to your mom and dad."

"Apologize?"

"Yes—say you're sorry."

"For joining the church?" His eyebrows jumped in disbelief.

"No—for going outside their will."

"I can't!"

"Let me ask you a question," I said. "Who do you want to please in your life—yourself or God?"

"God, I guess."

I reminded him of God's command to obey our parents, and asked him what he thought he needed to do.

"It's going to be so hard!" he stammered.

Once again I posed the question—"Who do you want to please?" Then we prayed together, and when we ended our conversation he felt ready to talk to his folks. Three weeks later, I stumbled into church twenty minutes late, and scooted into a pew near the back. As the service went on, I noticed that on the same pew were a man and a woman—and Todd.

After the service I greeted them, and later took Todd aside and asked, "Who are the people with you?"

"They're my parents," he said, and then told me what had happened: "I went home and did what you told me to do. I told Mom and Dad I would do whatever they wanted me to do, and that I would join whatever church they thought was best for me. After a while, they said that if my church taught me things that good, they'd join it too!

"Joe, they haven't been in the same church together in twenty-five years—until now!"

Some of the best things you can ever say to your parents are words like these: "Yes, sir," "Yes, ma'am," and "I'd be happy to." But watch out after you say them—your parents may have a heart attack!

A teenager from Colorado Springs shares the happiness found in putting back together a relationship with parents:

The main reason why I am writing is because of my parents. In your talks you really stress our friends and our relationships with our parents. Well my past was not a very pleasant one. I was drinking and smoking and smoking pot and I felt like I almost ripped my family into pieces. Well that one Sunday when we wrote our first letter home, I wrote my parents and thanked them for helping me through that time in my life. Now I have the greatest Christian family ever.

*A few months ago I wrote a song for my parents and I want to share it with you.*

The chorus to this teenager's song goes like this:

> They just want to give us all that they never had,
> to share with us their love and help us understand
> that we always have a friend,
> as long as we have them.

And these are the verses:

> Here's to the ones who've done all that they can.
> Here's to the ones who help us understand.
> They're the ones who know our feelings,
> the ones who are always there,
> the ones who've been here all along,
> the ones who really care.
>
> Here's to the ones who've taught us wrong from right.
> Here's to the ones who were with us day and night.
> They're the ones who've been so faithful,
> the ones who've helped us through,
> they will always love us
> no matter what we do.
>
> Here's to the ones who've made us who we are.
> Here's to the ones who are with us near or far.
> They're the ones who are so special
> that all of us need,
> for without them in our lives
> there would be no one to lead.

The letter ended with this P.S.: "I guess I just want to thank you for helping me realize that my parents really are the greatest!"

To wrap up this chapter, let me share with you a letter from a college girl in Texas whose dad had just died—a reminder to us all to realize and return our parents' love before it is too late:

I don't know why it still hurts when I know he's happier where he is! I loved him so much! I just feel I inadequately expressed it while he was here and I can't do anything about it. I've never cried this much or felt such a deep hurt until now. I guess I haven't had time to realize my loss.

Chapter 13

# FUTURE FRIEND

You can live for several weeks without food and several days without water. You can live for several minutes without oxygen.

But you can't really live for a second without hopes, dreams, and rainbows.

When kids tell me they're hurting, they tell me about things in their past. When they tell me they're doing fine, they tell me about things going on today. But when they're *EXCITED*, they talk about tomorrow — what they're living for, what they're looking forward to.

When God made you, He put three rainbows in your sky. The first and greatest rainbow is the one that never ends — the hope of eternal life. The second rainbow is life on earth — a lot of kids I know are finding this rainbow to be a fantastic adventure when they live life as God designed it to be lived. The third great rainbow — and it's worth your dreams and sincere prayers — is the day a prince (or princess) rides into your life, an event supercharged with as much expectation and beauty as any fairy tale ever told. Almost every teenager has the privilege to look forward to the opportunity to say "I do" to the wife or husband of his or her dreams. That lifelong wedding commitment is the birth of a friendship that cannot be fully described in the pages of this book.

It's so interesting how God provides great life rewards as our incentives to reach each of the three rainbows.

The incentive for the greatest rainbow is the choice between heaven and hell. Without a doubt, heaven is the all-time greatest place you could ever be. Hell no doubt is the worst place you could ever be — a place prepared for the devil and his fallen angels, a place so terrible that God desires to send absolutely no one there. People can get there only by their own choice, by choosing to reject God's payment for our sin through His Son.

The incentive for the second rainbow is the privilege of living life here in true freedom, the way it is supposed to be lived. Of course, we can use that freedom to destroy our minds and bodies with sin. After reading many of the letters in this book, you can see the warning signs of how sad that misuse of freedom can be.

The incentive for the third rainbow is the indescribable reward and privilege of being given an intimate friend to hold, to cherish, to respect, and to trust forever. You have the freedom to know this kind of relationship as you choose God's plan of happiness for your marriage — but it's the same freedom you can use to choose lust and immorality and instant cheap thrills that always result in hurt and broken relationships.

**Letters keep pouring in to me** about this, and more than anything else they say, "God is right. His Word is right. His way to live is the only way to really live. When I stray from His plan and go my own way, it hurts so badly."

Here's one of those many letters:

Ever since stacy's glorious wedding, I saw what I never could be— a virgin! I hate the feeling. Lately I could just cry all day. It's <u>so</u> depressing that because I had to be a stupid freshman I lost my little treasure chest. Luckily the key has been recovered and is saved for my future husband if I ever get married. I know that God has forgiven me, why can't I forgive myself? This week I've been acting weird because of it!"

In response to hearing the reality of God's plan for sex — that sex is to be saved for the "Prince" or "Princess" of your dreams, the one to whom you will give your life in marriage — a boy wrote me a short, blunt note of protest. It was scratched in pencil on the back of a yellow piece of paper:

SEX BRINGS TWO PEOPLE CLOSER TOGETHER.

I thought to myself, *He's so right — and he's so wrong.*

Two people who are intimately in love and joined in marriage do find a closeness in their intimacy that surpasses my ability to describe. It's so special it's worth *protecting* above every other physical aspect of your life.

In the premarital relationship, however, the closeness is a counterfeit. I can base this conclusion strictly on what teenagers for years have told me — they say the closeness is *temporary* only; while the separation it produces is *permanent.* The separation is from the person you experienced sex with, and all too often there's separation also from the one special relationship that is supposed to never end.

Why are so many more people choosing the sky without any rainbows? It's difficult to understand. Let me help you build a dream in your life for *your* future marriage and family.

I talk to more and more single people in their teens and twenties who are placing their future friend in his or her rightful place. Here are four encouraging letters I've received recently:

You showed me that I must give that aspect of my life (dating) to God; He will completely take over and lead me to the right friends. It is true, I would rather stay home on SaturdAY nights than to take the chance of hurting myself and my date.

Now I can pray for my future wife and pray that God will prepare us for each other. Also, I can just sit BACK and allow God to do with my life what he wants and I will make myself ready for my future. What a wonderful life God must have in store for me! I don't ever want to do anything to jeopardize that again. Since I have recommitted myself to Christ, my tears of guilt have turned to tears of joy!

□ □ □

"Ray loves the Lord and is such a leader. So many prayers have been answered through him, and it is such a testimony to the Lord. I'm not sure if I ever told you, but for three years I had not been in any serious dating relationship. I knew someday if I just trusted our Lord he would give me a perfect love. What an answer! Ray is coming home with me this Thanksgiving and Christmas. My parents love him dearly.

He's up for all Big 8 tackles and if he does get that and possibly go to pro ball, it's all a result of his tremendous love for our Father, and the Lord in return honoring Him."

□ □ □

"For awhile I was confused about sex. Tony was pushing me into doing it. After reading Looking For Love, I decided not to continue my relationship with Tony. I really want to wait until I get married to get involved with someone. I guess I always wanted to do that. Every time I feel like I might give in, I pick up my Bible and regain the perspective God wants me to have for my love life."

□ □ □

I pulled away and said no. Later on he told me he was very impressed that I said no because he said most girls wouldn't have the nerve. That made me feel so good because he realized I wasn't going to bow down to him because I was afraid I'd loose him. Later I told him I didn't think it was right and I didn't want to do that I just want him to respect me and treat me like I'm his little princess and he won't let anyone hurt me. I want him to know I'm a Christian and see Christ through my actions. I want us to have a good time without revolving our relationship around kissing and being totally serious.

**Is waiting for the best worth it?** Is your future best friend worth keeping your heart in a savings account, where it "grows with interest"?

Close your eyes and dream for a minute about her (or him). Ask that person if the intimacy you want to enjoy together forever is worth waiting for. Picture the unique closeness you're supposed to share on your honeymoon. Is a quick thrill worth spoiling that?

Look far into the future — at twenty, thirty, forty, fifty years together in the same home. Watch those little sons and daughters who share you and your mate's very likeness — watch them grow up, and see them come to you and wrap their arms around your neck, thanking you for being the best Mom and Dad in the world.

While writing this chapter, I'm also calling my happily married friends on the phone and asking them to describe for you what they're finding in their now-a-reality "future friend," the friend they waited for when they were teenagers:

> I believe my wife is the greatest gift God has given to me other than salvation. She is truly a helpmate in every sense of the word. She has met my every need, but more than anything else she has made me complete. *(They've been married 2 years)*

> I thank God daily for granting me the privilege to love and serve my husband, Brad. Our friendship abounds in joy and commitment beyond even all of my expectations for marriage. I know that this incredible blend of romance and responsibility could only be designed by our magnificent God. *(Married 2 years)*

> He's more than a friend. I have a dependable, trustworthy companion who is wholly mine.

He is my support. He doesn't even have to be there physically and I have him. I know what he would say, I know what he would do. I never, *never* have to say "Do you love me?" and "Are you my friend?" Through the years he has told me by his life and his words that he does and he is. He is forever telling me wonderful things about me. They're probably not all true, but he thinks they are. Even when we're across the room, it's like we're holding hands. He makes my life so fulfilling, so rich, so wonderful. *(Married 47 years)*

He was a true friend in high school who has become my committed lifetime friend. His love for me is the fullest expression of unconditional love. I know he respects me as an individual yet sees us as an inseparable team. He is my greatest counselor and encourager and my lover. *(Married 8 years)*

Joey is someone I can really be myself with. I can share my thoughts or feelings with him and not be afraid of rejection. It is a great security to know he'll always love me and support me. He's always there when I need him. He lives by the Bible, in that I feel like he loves me as Christ loves the church. He is a blessing from God. *(Married 3 years)*

Jeanie to me is my best friend, my buddy, and my lover all wrapped up in one package. It's neat because our love for one another, like God's love for us, always grows deeper and deeper — it never runs out. *(Married 3 years)*

Kris is all and more than I ever hoped to find in marriage. Psalm 37:4 says, "Delight yourself in the Lord; and He will give you the desires of your heart." Never did I expect the

Lord to give me the desires of my heart concerning a husband — but He did! Kris makes my heart smile! *(Married $1^1/_2$ years)*

I can't begin to tell you how special my Little Honey is. Picture the best friend you could ever have and multiply that by ten. That gives you an idea how neat my wife is. She without a doubt is the biggest blessing in my life. I can't thank the Lord enough for her. *(Married $1^1/_2$ years)*

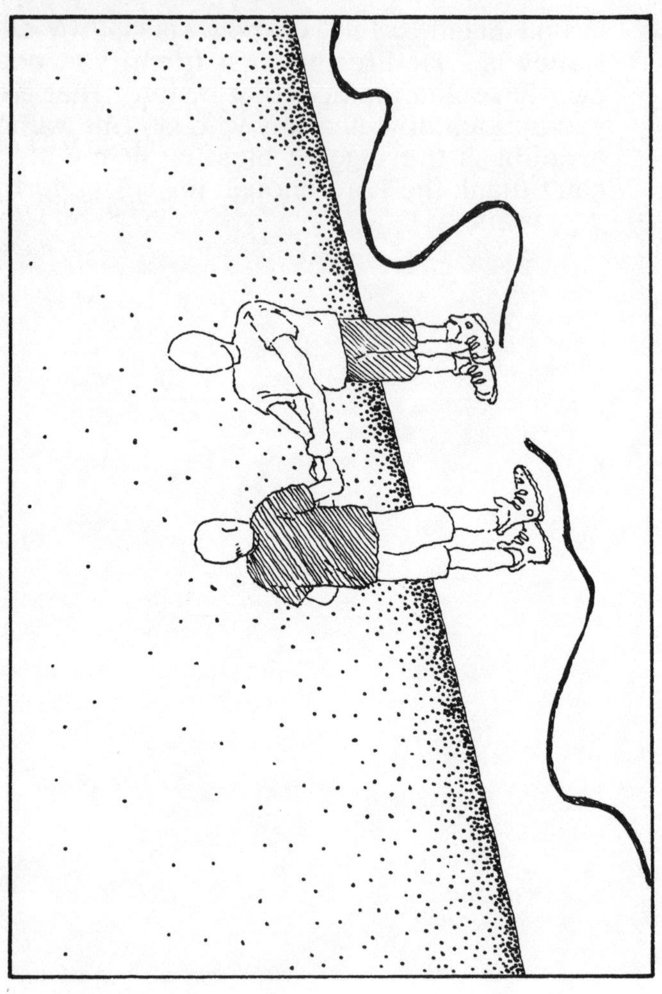

# Chapter 14

# FOREVER FRIENDS

Think about it: If I told you I loved you and called you my friend, you could expect me to give you my very best. I couldn't give you any more — but I shouldn't give you any less.

Look at the following list of things people often do to or for their "friends." If you were asked to rank them on a one-to-ten scale — with one being the worst thing possible, and ten the best — your list would probably look much like mine, because all people have the same basic needs:

① Saying or doing things that would lead the person into hell.

② Gossiping about the friend and destroying his or her reputation.

③ Being dishonest and building up a friend's false hopes.

④ Leading a friend into bad habits with drugs, premarital sex, or alcohol.

⑤ Using the friend for what you can get from him.

*(True friendship begins here:)*

⑥ Saying a kind word or giving a gift to help make someone's day.

⑦ Being there when someone needs you.

⑧ Helping a friend find a positive solution to a tough lifestyle problem — helping out through your advice and through the example of your own way of life.

⑨ Loving a friend no matter what he or she does.

⑩ Helping a friend discover the greatest gift anyone could ever receive — a relationship with Jesus Christ.

How few "eight," "nine," and "ten" friendships there are! I think they're a scarce commodity because it isn't easy to be that kind of friend. To stand up and always do what is right for a friend takes the courage of a 160-pound defensive cornerback taking on a 220-pound fullback crashing through the line.

"Eight," "nine," and "ten" friends get hurt sometimes. Sometimes they have to stand alone against the "popular" trends. They will even get laughed at, and sometimes left out of certain cliques and parties.

But they have no regrets — and no guilt. And God has all of eternity to commend and reward them for being the way they are.

Is it worth it? I haven't been to heaven yet, but someday, when I get there, by God's grace I'll scream out across the thunder, "YES! It is worth it!"

You don't have to wait until heaven, though. I find a small piece of heaven on this earth every day. I find it day after day and night after night in the eyes of my wife, as we laugh together, pray together, cry together, and grow together. Even through misunderstandings we come out with a greater friendship than when the conflict began. I find it also in the eyes of a son or daughter who squeezes an arm around my neck and whispers in my ear, "I love you, Daddy."

**How do you handle** the sometimes difficult situation when you begin to change and your "friends" are still the same? When I was seventeen, I had a "best friend" who was pressuring me hard to "get wilder" while he ridiculed me for my Christian faith. A real friend gave me a passage out of God's love letter that really made a difference in my life. I reread it often:

> You have had enough in the past of the evil things the godless enjoy — sex sin, lust, getting drunk, wild parties, drinking bouts, and the worship of idols, and other terrible sins. Of course, your former friends will be very surprised when you don't eagerly join them any more in the wicked things they do, and they will laugh at you in contempt and scorn. But just remember that they must face the Judge of all, living and dead; they will be punished for the way they have lived. (1 Peter 4:3-5, *The Living Bible*)

By helping me realize that *my* judgment would be for how *I* lived, and *my friends'* judgment would be for how *they* lived, this passage helped me begin a change I am still pursuing (and benefitting from) today. It has been so much FUN watching God give so much attention to someone as ordinary as I am, as He continues to mold me into the happy man He wants me to be.

Today I have a tremendously uplifting Christian friendship with the guys I call my "buddies." Even when I fail them, they stay loyal to me. They know my many faults and love me anyway.

God also has given me the thrill of learning how to love others enough to help point them to their truly Best Friend. My heart hits the sky when a letter like this one comes across my desk:

No one has ever touched me or affected me like you did. I honestly do not think I would have accepted Jesus Christ into my heart if you had not been there. The greatest day of my life was March 23, 1983, when I accepted Jesus into my life. You were by my side that night with encouragement while I was doubtful and with patience while I cried my eyes out. I can never thank you enough for taking time to talk to me when I really needed you. You helped to fill my life with God.

The same kind of "ten" friendship can go on at age 14...

Thank you so much for the picture of Tom and me. I love it! It is my favorite picture. I have it in a big frame on my desk so I see it a lot. It made me realize how blessed I am to have such a great friend like her! Last night was the first time I have ever opened up to my friends about the Lord! I am so glad I finally did! I explained to her about how I needed to depend on the Lord more and spend more time with him. We had the greatest talk we've ever had. I'm so glad I have finally got it out in the open. I am so happy now.

And at age 17...

My best friend for the weekend made semi-finals in the pageant also. So that was really neat. She placed sixth and I got seventh. The relationships I've made seems like they had been nurtured for years. It's neat to see how quickly God can bond people.

The one thing that made my weekend was that following the pageant we were all just talking and eating and I was talking to two girls for over half an hour about who God is and all that he has to offer. They both became Christians. It was so neat because I realized how important my lifestyle is.

And at 19...

I fell in love with Tina. We didn't have any sexual problems as she was very old fashioned and I had Christ, except that He was lost somewhere between the Y and Z part of my alphabetized priorities. Finally last Sunday, I rededicated my life to Christ. I gave it all up to Him, even my relationship with Tina. I think that was the hardest thing that I ever had to do. I love her so very much. I love everything she does, says, or thinks. Just being in the same room with her fills me with unbelievable joy. I have never in my life experienced such an outstanding and exceptional love for any human being. I had to choose, so I gave it all up to Christ as I knew that I could no longer go on in such a way.

We were in Austin last weekend. On our drive back, I shared it all with her. Surprisingly enough, she wanted me to help her to discover the meaning of what I had done and help her to live a "better life." After three and four hour nightly discussions, Bible in hand, Tina finally accepted Christ last night. I am so excited that I shared that beautiful moment with her. She is so excited about her new life. God has been so good to me. He has given Tina and me so much. We love each other completely unconditionally."

Let me close this book by sharing with you perhaps my favorite true story I've ever heard, outside of the Bible.

Gene Stallings, head football coach of the Phoenix Cardinals, is a true friend of mine. He helped me through the roughest time of my life several years ago. He has a captivating personality. When he speaks, I listen intensely.

We were in his pickup one autumn day going to see a boy in the hospital. He pulled up to a stoplight and looked over at me with those big brown eyes, and said with seriousness, "I want to tell you a story — it's a good one, and it's true. You listening?"

"Yes, sir, I'm listening."

The light turned green. As we pulled through the intersection he began, and as he continued he would look at me every few seconds to impress a certain point.

"I was going to speak at a banquet the other night," he said, "and I was sitting in the car with an older gentleman. Between us on the seat was a very old scrapbook that had been in this man's family for generations. As I flipped through the pages of it, I came across a very interesting letter."

Coach Stallings looked at me intensely and added, "It wasn't a copy of the letter — it was the real thing."

I squirmed in my seat.

"The letter was from a 19-year-old boy named Sam Davis. Here's what he wrote:

> Dear Mom and Dad,
>
> Tomorrow I will be hanged. It's nothing you've done but I've gotten into trouble here in the war and they're going to hang me.
>
> Love, Sam

"I couldn't wait to find out more about this Sam Davis, so I went to the history books and found out that he was a young Confederate spy in the Civil War, assigned to go behind the Union Army's lines and gather information. On one such spy mission he ran into another 19-year-old from the Union Army and became friends."

Now Coach Stallings looked at me to see if I

caught his emphasis on the last phrase. I had.

"Those two 19-year-old friends stayed together for several days. As Sam was leaving to go back to his army, the Union soldier gave him some outdated maps of Union troop movements and said, 'Sam, these maps are no longer accurate, but put them into your saddlebags and take them to your general. They'll think you did a good job over here and give you a promotion.'

"Sam was probably laughing to himself as he went away. But while he was trying to cross the front lines, he was apprehended by a Union guard who went through his papers and found the maps. 'Where did you get the maps, son?' he asked.

" 'I'm not going to tell you.'

" 'You'll tell us all right!' He had Sam locked up.

"After a few days passed, the gallows were set up for Sam's hanging. Guards came to his cell to get him, and they made him ride to the gallows on his coffin, which was secured on a horse-drawn wagon.

"In front of the gallows they stopped, and a Union general approached the frightened young teenager. 'What's your name, son?' he asked.

" 'Sam Davis, sir.'

" 'Do you see those gallows? They're for you.'

" 'Yes, sir.'

" 'If you'll tell me where you got the maps, I won't hang you.'

"Sam replied, 'I can't tell you.'

" 'What do you mean you can't tell me? Didn't you hear what I just offered you?'

"Sam paused, then answered, 'I got the maps from a <u>friend</u>, sir, and I'm not going to tell you who he is.'

"The general looked intently into the teenager's eyes. 'Look, son,' he said. 'You're nineteen years old and have a long life ahead of you. I don't want to hang you. I just want to know where you got the maps. If you'll just tell me who gave them to you, I'll personally escort you back across the lines to safety.

*Where did you get the maps?'*

"With the boldness of a much older warrior, Sam Davis looked into the general's face and said, 'Sir, I'd die a thousand deaths before I'd deny my friend, and I am disappointed you would ask me to do it.' "

Coach Stallings stopped the truck, leaned his head toward me, and said, "Now that's true friendship. *'I'd die a thousand deaths before I'd deny my friend.'* — Joe, that's true friendship."

I got the message. And I'll never forget the story.

**As I lay down my pen**, let me ask you to take a minute, put your head back, and close your eyes and dream a little with me. Let each of your friends — past, present, and future — pass before you in your mind, and put each one to the test: What kind of friends are they? What kind of friends do you want them to be? What kind of friend do they find in you?

This may be one of the best opportunities you'll ever have to talk to God about where you are going with your life and what kind of friend you're going to go with. Invite Him into your heart and mind — even into the area that controls your many friendships — and let Him have control.

As you put Him into the driver's seat of your life, you can expect your friendships to take on a whole new dimension — both now and forever.

**Finally** — I want to thank you for the opportunity to share this book and my life with you.

Joe

# About the Author

Together with his remarkable family, **Joe White** runs Kanakuk-Kanakomo Kamps in Missouri's Ozark Mountains, a Christian sports camp complex that ranks as one of the largest of its kind in the world. The camp's staff each summer includes more than a thousand college students and collegiate and professional athletes.

■■■

Tim Hansel (author of *What Kids Need Most in a Dad, You Gotta Keep Dancin',* and *Holy Sweat* ) says this about Joe:

> Joe White is like E.F. Hutton to me. When he speaks, I *listen.* I listen because his vast experience with hundreds of thousands of kids has enabled him to put his fingers on the very pulse of our nation. I listen because he is a man after God's own heart. I listen because he has a heart too big for his body — especially when it comes to kids and their families. I listen most of all because he listens to God, and when he speaks it's as if God's echo is resounding from the pages.
>
> Joe White is one of God's real men. He has a raging love affair with God and with kids from all over the world — and he wants to give each of them an opportunity to be their very best.
>
> Joe White is one of a kind....

**Joe's other books—**

*for teens:*

LOOKING FOR LOVE
— IN ALL THE WRONG PLACES

WHO'S NUMBER ONE?
— HOW TO BE A CHRISTIAN IN A ME-FIRST WORLD

*for parents:*

WHAT KIDS WISH PARENTS KNEW ABOUT PARENTING

HOW TO BE A HERO TO YOUR TEENAGER